from heroin to heaven

The raw and honest collection of entries from an addicted, bipolar mind who finds the way out... once and for all.

by

Mariah Noelle Freeman

ACKNOWLEDGMENTS

I want to acknowledge my husband who lovingly encourages me in my walk with God and who has supported my efforts in publishing my story.

A special thank you to my parents and two older siblings who have loved me unconditionally throughout many years of hardship caused by my actions.

Thanks to Bernie and Cathy Gillott who spent endless hours working on the formatting of this manuscript, even in the midst of their busy travel schedules.

Thank you to Kristy S. Johnson for editing my mess of words she turned into a manuscript.

And finally, I want to thank my beloved boss Don Wilkerson for his godly mentorship in my life and for his efforts in the advising of this book.

DEDICATION

This book is dedicated to the addicted, the depressed, the lonely, the prostitutes and the sick. You are the reason I wrote my story. May you find the love, peace and rest for your soul that you have been searching for.

What People Are Saying About

FROM HEROIN TO HEAVEN

∞

Powerful, raw and passionate. I was on a roller coaster of emotions- one moment I was laughing, and then crying as Mariah shared her story. Her ability to tell her story with so much honesty gives others hope in their own journey. As I read the book, I remembered watching Mariah take this journey and all I could say was, "Thank You, Jesus!" This is a must-read.

-**Beth Greco**, Vice President of the Walter Hoving Home

Mariah's story of grace is a much needed voice of light in the dark world of addiction. I challenge you to step into her story and be confronted with the same power of grace that drastically set her free.

-**Will Kitchen**, Pastor/ Teacher/ Fellow Grace-Receiver

For all those who wonder if God still works miracles today, you can look no further than the life of Mariah Freeman. This volume is a must-read for every believer who yearns to reach those with life-controlling problems; and for anyone caught in addiction and heartache, who believes they can never be free! "He whom the son sets free, is free indeed!" Mariah is a living example of restoration that only comes with living your life for Christ.

-**Dr. Jesse Owens**, Missionary/ Evangelist/ Brooklyn Teen Challenge Recruiter

Wow! FROM HEROIN TO HEAVEN is the reality that if we could save ourselves, we wouldn't need a savior. Reading Mariah's journal entries from her mind, her heart and her soul challenges my faith to hold tighter to God's hand and trust His unfailing Word because there is no place too dark or too far that God's love can't reach.

-**Ashley Brown**, the Brooklyn Tabernacle Dance Ministry Leader

I'm not a big reader, but I started reading Mariah's testimony and couldn't put it down. I read it straight through, got on my knees and worshipped God for His grace and mercy in His children's lives. Thank you Mariah!

-**Nathan Lloyd-Jones**, Missionary in Honduras

Viewing life through the lens of brokenness and betrayal is a tortured existence. In this book, Mariah gives a fresh, passionate, vulnerable look at life and addiction through the feelings, observations and journal entries of her journey. A chronicle of her life of addiction to a victorious and abundant life; this remarkably candid and thought-provoking view, through the looking-glass of her pain, is an open promise to those that have ever struggled and wondered if there is any hope. This is more than one woman's testimony of freedom from addictions, eating disorders and overwhelming pain... it is an open promise that anyone who comes to God with their shopping list of "impossibilities" has an invitation to a miracle. If He did it for her, God can do it for you.

-**Pastor Bernie Gillott**, Global Evangelism Coordinator, Teen Challenge

FOREWARD

All my adult life I have been surrounded by the amazing life changes of those enslaved by addiction. A few testimonies and stories stand out among them. FROM HEROIN TO HEAVEN is one of them.

Mariah was my administrative Assistant for four years following her graduation from the Teen Challenge Walter Hoving Home Women's Program. As we worked together I got to know how crazy she is for Jesus- in a very powerful and practical way. I learned the depths of the living hell that heroin addiction took her through and as a result the scripture, *"where sin abounds grace abounds so much more"* became a reality to me as never before.

Mariah grew up in a good home with good parents, but she made some bad choices in her early teens. These decisions turned her into someone and something no one should ever have to experience- as you can read in this sobering yet Christ exalting book. These writings from her past journal entries are real and raw as are the expression of her feelings at the time she was going through such deep darkness.

As I got to know her during her work for me and Brooklyn Teen Challenge and learned where and what she'd come from, I was inspired even more to reach young girls and women who were like she once was.

If you, your family or your friends have been touched by addiction in any way I highly recommend this book. It will give you hope you can pass along to others.

If you or others you know might question whether Jesus is real or relevant for today, this book is filled with signs and wonders about God's power.

While some would consider Mariah's life a return to "normal life"… she is now a wife, mother of a beautiful daughter and lives a new and vibrant life. For her, every day is a miracle because of what God has done in her life.

-**Don Wilkerson**, Co-Founder of Teen Challenge and President of Brooklyn Teen Challenge

TABLE OF CONTENTS

∞Important Note to the Reader on the next page∞

Note to the Reader

People often ask me, "What happened to you to make you do the things you did?" The answer is nothing really *happened* to me. I was never sexually abused as a child, my parents loved me very much and I had a "normal" and happy childhood. I believe the reason I fell so hard and so fast was because I left the path that leads to life and I turned my back on God... I suffered greatly as a result.

Precious stones are found in the dirt, cut and then polished using intense friction. Now I am not calling myself precious, but Jesus sure does. He says, *"You are precious and honored in my sight, and I love you...."* (Isaiah 43:4) Let that piece of scripture resonate with you as you thumb through these honestly written pages.

My life now is *heaven*. It wasn't always so. Around the age of seven I began to obsessively count things. I would find myself feeling uneasy if I couldn't finish counting whatever it was that I was fixated on at the moment (lines, patterns, tile floors, etc.). I also struggled with obsessive thoughts and fears. These obsessions eventually turned into impulsive behaviors that I had a hard time controlling. By the age of twelve I began drinking, smoking and longing for peace. At age thirteen I was onto my first treatment of psychotropic medication following my first suicide attempt.

The life of an addict is severe. It is torture. Addicts do things most people would never dream of; lying, stealing, begging and murdering- just to name a few of the things addicts regretfully do. We do these things to *get what we want or think we need.* I've learned that selfishness is the farthest thing from God... and the farthest thing from wholeness.

I think addiction is a complex demon but the remedy is simpler than we all think.

∞

John 11:4 Jesus said, *"This sickness is not unto death, but for the glory of God, that the Son of God may be glorified through it."*

No amount of filthy addictions can scare off Jesus. I was the dirtiest, the filthiest and the farthest away from being "saved." But there is no battle too strong for our God. In fact the battle *belongs* to Him. Fighting the overwhelming power of addiction and mental illness with our own willpower is about as possible as a cow jumping over the moon. I have tried fighting this demon on my own. I have tried and tried and *tried...* and kept failing.

When we come to Jesus with our heavy burdens of pain and regret, He readily takes them. He washes us clean with His blood. He forgives our every sin... our *every* sin. We can experience joy as our sin dies and we are bound in slavery no more. We must only *believe* that He is.

He is waiting to talk with you... He is listening.

I love this promise in Exodus 14:13;

Do not be afraid. Stand firm and you will see the deliverance the Lord will bring you today...

∞

These are the journal entries, thoughts and reflections over the past twenty years of my life as a "good Christian girl," to a rebel, to an addict, to a prostitute; all the way back to *my heaven*, which is, and always will be, my relationship with Jesus Christ.

∞

introduction

A poem, a prayer and a Psalm

Slipping is what I feel most days.

The scary panic of attack on my mind.

Tears are verging

Submerging my inner most being.

The tears well up, well up, well up

And gush out.

I count the square patterns on the floor.

And I count the squares inside the
squares and I don't like uneven numbers.

Except seven.

And I sometimes like the number three.

The Lord is with me- yes.

But the obsessions and dismembered
thoughts are with me as well.

God- bring me back to simplicity;

To being a child.

To sitting on a ledge with my feet dangling
and laughing...

At the ducks fighting each other.

God,

I believe everything happens for a reason,
then again, why am I still alive?

Why do I continue to stab myself in the
back? I am my own worst enemy. And I
hate myself for everything I've put my
family through. I'm such a horrible person; I
really don't deserve to live.

God, please take me, please let me leave
this world, I beg You. Save me from the
cold hell I've been living, from the lies, the
anger and the hatred I have stored up in
me. I want to pass on...

I'm too old and gray for this life. My life is
meaningless without You, God. I feel I

have drifted away, to someone I am not, to

a place I don't belong.

Someone help me.

God? Where are You? Please take me

with You... wherever You are.

I will not die; instead, I will live to tell what the Lord has done. The Lord has punished me severely, but he did not let me die.

∞Psalm 118:17-18 (NLT)∞

aftermath

I think we all suffer from blindness at times. Life is a constant journey of trying to open your eyes. I'm just beginning my journey, and my eyes aren't fully open yet.

∞Olivia Thirlby∞

The eyes that stared at me from across my desk were glazed over and bloodshot.

I ask her, "How do you feel about your pregnancy?"

She replies with a shrug.

I try again, "You look disconnected... are you feeling numb?"

She responds, "Yea... numb. So do ya'll do abortions here?"

I nod in empathy and understanding to her desire to run away from her pregnancy. My eyes squint as I try to reach into her soul and shake her with love and warning. I already know she's made her mind up on aborting the baby.

"No. I'm sorry. We do not perform abortions here. But I want to help you through this in any way I can."

Her eyes seem to moisten a bit, but she remained steadfast in her silence. Internally I ask God to speak to her and to please give me words. I go on to tell her my own story, when I had an abortion. I tell her of the psychological pain, the guilt, the shame and the utter dark remorse I felt when I finally realized what I had done.

She asks surprisingly, "You mean *you've* had an abortion? Why did you?"

I respond, "Yes, when I was 17 years old. I was already hooked on cocaine, weed and alcohol at that point... I broke up with the boyfriend who got me pregnant and I felt like I was all alone. I didn't feel ready for a baby. I was worried about what everyone would say about me... the list goes on and on. But basically it boils down to the fact that because I was so detached from reality and not wanting to hear the truth about what was happening in my womb- that I let fear and lies take over my mind.

She stares at me and I can tell she is at least listening. Her friend that she brought with her is slouched down on the couch as she's texting on her iPhone.

I go on, "But do you know that God has loved me regardless of my poor choices? And that all He wants from me is to acknowledge Him and be in a relationship with Him?"

She nods and says she knows who Jesus is.

I assure her of His love and care for her and that He is with her every step of the way. I encourage her in the love of Christ and that He wants so badly to help her through this decision. I ask if I could give her a hug and she readily agrees. She and her friend leave my office and I stare off in wonder and amazement; that numb and confused girl was me just 13 years ago as I walked into a pregnancy center. However the center that I chose to walk into was called Planned Parenthood. And their goal was not to love, counsel and educate women about the harmful effects of abortion- but it was to slyly cover up the gruesome facts and "help" women get rid of their "problem."

Later that evening, I wrapped myself in my husband's strong, safe arms and expressed my concern for the girl who earlier came to see me.

It sometimes seems like a vague and distant memory when I think about my past...

thirteen

In that day the lovely young women and strong young men will faint because of thirst.

∞**Amos 8:13**∞

The following entries were found in my journal from when I was thirteen years old.

Today was another horrible day. In 2nd period I went to the bathroom and took 8 Advil and 3 Benadryl. I wanted to get all my problems off my mind and I can barely move- I'm feeling so weird. In school I couldn't move either and I just threw up a little. The pills did not make my pain go away. I'm still so sad and alone. My life right now is really hard and confusing and stressful. I hate my life.

∞

I was thinking of killing myself in church today... I do that a lot- think about that. What is there to live for anyway? I want to die so badly.

∞

Well I can tell you that my life is very, very disturbed and something is obviously distorted here. I just can't figure it out. I want to die so bad, so bad. God, I want to freaking die. My eye twitches and I get all these anger spasms all the time. Maybe it's because I think everyone hates me. I am going to keep trying to kill myself. I always picture myself dead and how I died and everyone is always laughing at me. Like in my dreams, I dream that I die all the time and that everyone is trying to figure out why and I'm in a cage- it's yellow and rusty and I'm trying to break free. But nothing works. Nothing works! I keep screaming until I can't scream anymore and I keep feeling like I need to die to get the pain over with. I want to die- I have such a strong desire to die.

∞

Last night was so weird. I went to the counseling room before 8th period and they called the police on me. They took me and my friend (who I just cut my wrists with) to Park Ridge hospital in separate ambulances. They put me in a white room all by myself for hours. It was about 9pm when I saw a shrink. We talked about my problems and that helped some. I'm just full of problems and depression.

∞

Today I was told by my principal that I wasn't allowed to go to the 8th grade

Washington trip because I am too unstable. I wanted to go so bad! How could people do this to me? Shit... I hate my life.

∞

Today I feel like I'm not suicidal anymore! My life was such a spiral going downward and it took a long time to get back out of that and see the light. But I even stopped smoking!

∞

Good things don't last long I guess. I went to the beach today and cut my wrist... I got so mad because this guy I am going out with told all his friends we had sex- and we didn't! I hate my life so much, so much, so much. Why can't I be perfect like my sister? I feel like she never has any problems.

P.S. If anyone reads this I want them to know that I killed myself due to: harassment, accusations of dirty things, nothing going right and my own drive of adrenaline to hate myself because of my appearance and I have no real friends. Well, I love everyone and I always have loved the ones I say that I hate- but that's only because I was caught up in all *their* hate.

∞

sick

Around the age of fifteen the sickness of addiction and mental illness grabbed ahold of me. The following are entries written during several years on and off at hospitals, inpatient treatment centers, detoxification centers and throughout seasons of homelessness.

Once again... pain. Pain so deep I can't breathe can't hear and can't taste... only feeling is a feeling of loneliness and pain. This place is a jail cell... dirty bathrooms, flies and sharing my room with 3 other girl addicts. Luckily I have nice girls with me and I just found out we get one minute phone calls. Gee, a whole minute, how thoughtful. I'm in a place with disgusting people and gross attitudes. Can I handle it? Right now I can't handle much of anything. I've been crying all day, so exhausted and so tired. I don't have a pillow so I can't sleep well, there are holes in my sheets, the bed is made of ripped plastic and there is too much light coming from the window. I'm still waiting for my medicine.

I'm so alone. I'm so scared, so lost. I'm so
alone.

∞

Today I actually feel like I'm already dead.
I feel like I'm seeing myself act out a fake
life. I hate who I am and all the
opportunities I passed in life... all the
wrong decisions I've made. Why do I still
pity me? What's so bad in my life? My mom
was right about how I've kept myself from
growing up... I've always depended on
someone else and I feel so trapped
because of that. I'm trapped in my own
head and will never get out, because this is
what God chose for me- if there is a god.
That's another thing I'm not so sure
about... we all used to go to church every

Sunday- rain or shine- and now none of us go anymore and I don't know anything anymore. Nothing. My life is a disgrace, a total waste. I feel like a thirteen year old all over again. I'm so lost and scared and hate myself. I don't know what's right and what's wrong, what's up and what's down. My world is like a Picasso painting.

∞

I hate that I killed my baby. I hate that I tried killing myself so many times and it never worked! I hate how my mind works that I'm so depressed every second of every day. I hate myself for getting addicted to freaking heroin. I never would have though a well- raised, happy, sweet child that I once was would turn into *this*!

This: being a nasty, stupid, ugly and worthless girl. I hate how I let everyone down. I hate how bad I hurt them. I hate how I let guys take advantage of me. I hate all the lies, the cheats, the discords I've caused. Being here in this detox- alone- just really makes me see what I've become and it really, really sickens me. IT SICKENS ME.

∞

Today my nurse technician happened to be a girl I went to East Ridge Performing Arts high school with. She is such a sweetheart. It kind of depressed me because look where she is and look where I am. I even said that to her and she smiled at me and said, "Mariah, you're doing the right thing and taking the first step to getting better and that's all that matters right now!" Familiar faces in the hospital always bring joy... especially when they have something nice to say.

∞

I hate myself for being sick. I hate everything about me. I want to slice my skin open so bad. I hate my life. *I hate it.* I want to die so bad. *Please God, take me soon... I can't suffer like this for much longer. I just can't do it.*

∞

John Norris Inpatient Treatment Center

Today is the first day of the rest of my life. It's my second run at Norris Rehab and I'm praying to God it's my last. My parents have given up on me and they should. I have given up as well and the addiction took the wheel and drove me to insanity. I need God in my life again... it's too hard without Him. I can't change my thinking with *my* thinking. So I'm asking God today for help and for strength.

∞

Today is a pretty good day, I'd say. Had some good therapy and saw that Christian lady from last year who gives out Bibles and candy. She gave me a hug; it was nice to see her smiling, warm eyes. My recovery is very important to me, but I didn't hit rock bottom this time around, or an extreme 'low.' That kind of scares me, actually. I do not trust myself at all when I get out of here. I really have to keep checking myself. I need to be one hundred percent honest and check my motives all the time for the rest of my life- damn- I hate this disease.

∞

Today we had no Alcoholics Anonymous meetings, so I went to a Bible study instead. I need more God in my life. Thought I had Him last time I got help, and maybe I did, but I lost Him and it's all my fault.

∞

Today I'm reflecting on what happened yesterday. After group therapy I cried a lot and for the first time in a while. It felt good, but at the same time I was confused as to why exactly I cried. I think I was upset about not having my family and not having their support like I did last time. I told the counselor today that my thoughts are extremely jumbled, like a jungle is going on in my head. Hopefully it will settle down and clear up a little when the meds kick in.

∞

Today the staff did room searches and my coffee and sugar that I stashed is now gone! Oh well, at least I didn't get written up this time. Sarah just dropped off information about this program called The Walter Hoving Home... it seems like a huge commitment. I just don't know if I'm ready for that yet...

∞

I actually spoke and said what was bothering me in group therapy today. But only because the counselor called on me to speak what was on my mind. I really need to work on my issues more thoroughly. Maybe I'm scared I'm gonna be judged or something. Last night I was thinking about when I was with Mac buying heroin and he ran into the little boy while driving my car and I was in the passenger seat screaming for him to stop the car so we could check on the boy. But there was a horrible snow storm and we had to get out of the drug area quickly. I remember screaming and screaming for Mac to stop the car but the need for heroin trumped every situation...

no matter how traumatizing the consequence.

∞

Well it seems like things might be worth living for. I have a lot of hard work ahead of me and am getting anxious but at the same time getting mentally prepared. To change the mind is a very hard task. Not only do you need to let go of the past, you also need to accept and learn to move forward.

∞

So many questions left unanswered... why is it when you need to be alone somehow you can't, but if you need to be with people that's even harder? Also, why do I always pick the horrible men? Men who abuse me mentally, physically and emotionally? Or who steal from me, lie to me, even violate me? I am about fed up with Rochester and everyone in this God forsaken city. There is definitely something wrong with me besides being an addict and besides having mental illnesses. What if all your friends are toxic, bad influences? And what if you pushed your family all away? Who do you turn to? I need help... I just need to pace myself... I am stressed out a little because I have to be out of my state- funded apartment soon and I don't have anywhere to go.

∞

Living in a State-Funded Apartment

I have much experience with going crazy... it comes out of nowhere and is so very powerful. Flashbacks keep coming; of being tied down at the hospital and trying to squirm my way out of it... a big, intimidating security man throw me down on the hospital bed because I kept fighting everyone... just to name a few. I'm heading there again... these demons inside me are taking over and have full range and control of my actions and behaviors. I guess writing about it is the only way to get this out... to release the evil. But what if I'm not good enough to be saved from this? My behaviors are bad, so I must be bad. Right now I'm waiting for this guy to come over. He will give me what I want and then ask for sex. If I can get high enough I probably will let him sleep with me. He has control over me because he has money, a car, a way to get me to my drugs and all of that which I do not have. All I am is a heroin addicted sex slave.

∞

I feel as though a thousand pound elephant just stepped on my heart. The panic of my heart is beating to its sick tune of painful memories. It feels as though I have no control and the world, as I know it, is coming to a dreadful end. I think it may be this new medication they have me on... some sort of hormone I have to take for ten days and then hopefully I'll get my period. My period stops a lot because of the drugs and I don't take very good care of myself. Obviously.

∞

Why can't I ever sleep? I hate my life, I hate it with such a passion. I am cursed; I am stuck with this mind and this body. I think there comes a point in everyone's life where enough is just enough! There's only so much we can all take. It feels like everything at once is coming to a forceful halt. My whole life is just crumbling and I mean that literally and figuratively. My hopes and dreams, my family and friends all have stopped in mid-air... suspended in time. Have you ever felt like you were flying in the clouds and had no fathom of what time is was or where you were? So when a crisis happens... what are your coping strategies? It's imperative to have these skills. I am someone who has been through what seems like a million classes of such skill-cultivating lessons. So when my 5th mental hygiene arrest happened last weekend, you can imagine or guess maybe that this shouldn't have happened to a young, semi-educated, "smart" girl. I need to get away, I need to fly away. I need to go... it's in my blood to follow the wind.

∞

Sojourner Halfway House

I feel so sick to my stomach today. I almost puked and my head hurts and everything is just uncomfortable. I hate it when I'm nauseous. *God please help me to feel better just for a little bit. I am so sick. Thank You.*

∞

Well things have calmed down a bit at this halfway house... but someone keeps stealing my cereal. That's why I keep my cigarettes, money and candy in my backpack locked up with a padlock. You can't trust a single soul in this freaking house. They will act friendly in your face then talk about you as soon as you leave the room. I have gotten a lot better with sticking to myself, staying in my room and keeping out of the gossip. I got way too involved when I first moved in and as a result I got really hurt and ended up in the middle of lies. The fact is everyone here talks about everyone here. The solution is to not talk about anyone and to never let your guard down.

∞

I love my nieces. They are too cute for words, I would do anything for them. I'm supposed to go hang out with them today because my sister is coming to get me! Ugh, Dora's child won't stop crying, I can't even think. And she just keeps yelling at her and the child keeps crying and AH! I know I'm not a mother, but that is really rude to have your child screaming while someone is on the phone... she could at least have taken her out of the room! Just breathe Mariah, breathe. The moms around here really do not know how to parent. And that is evident because they are stuck in this place with me, this halfway house and here I am judging. Ironic isn't it? I can't wait to have babies... I think I'll be an excellent mom. Well I better go wait for my big sissy!

∞

It seems like this life will never end... this rehab life. I want to lose- no I *will* lose fifteen pounds soon. I've been eating extremely healthy now and it feels good to do that. This methadone makes you gain like a hundred pounds. I feel like I'm gonna be stuck in the system my whole life.

∞

The other night I couldn't even stand up cuz my chest and tummy hurt so bad. At 8:20pm I just passed out. Yesterday, I had the worst withdrawal because I accidently sold Joy 70 milliliters of methadone instead of 30, but she was nice enough to give me five bucks for that. I know I shouldn't be selling methadone, but what else am I supposed to do for money? On the first I sell my food stamps just to get some loot for cigarettes and clothes cuz it's getting colder out so I need warm clothes that I can fit into since I'm so fat.

∞

Why do I keep seeing myself die? Maybe I'm going to soon. I think I am- I'm almost convinced. The only reason I don't go ahead and do it now is because everyone says that you automatically go to hell if you commit suicide. What do they know? I think I need a good cry. I haven't cried in forever.

∞

Today I still have a headache from two days ago and I thought maybe I would feel better and it would go away but it didn't. so I went to talk to Miss Wendy and she seemed real mad that I didn't think I could go to the Eastman Theater that night with the rest of the house. She said, "Well, Miss Andrea paid $30 a ticket for us to go to this event and she's gonna be real mad that she wasted that money on you." Then Miss Henley said, "They probably gonna take away your weekends off property for not wanting to go to this event."

Gee, thanks. Not like I have enough problems and stress in my life right now, so let's adds a side of punishment and guilt to the mix!

∞

Who knows what'll happen. Today they took away our snacks because apparently someone stole two slabs of ribs from the fridge?! *God, I just want OUT.*

∞

I am really unsettled. I wish I was rich and living in California. But I would still have problems. I was thinking about just taking like forty sleeping pills. It would be painless. What if I go to hell? I don't even understand the heaven and God thing. I mean... why would He want us to go through some of the things we go through? I think if there is a God, He just wanted to create a world to entertain Himself. Maybe He was bored. But if that's what it is, I'll be so mad. I feel too real to be a puppet, but then again sometimes I don't feel real at all. I've reached that one moment when you're lying in bed and think to yourself, "Who am I? How did I get here? Where do I go when I die?" Such questions wouldn't be asked if they didn't have an answer. I'm too worthless to go anywhere in this life. I bet I'll succeed a lot better someplace else... somewhere other than this cruel, cold, lonely and evil world. I want to be with my baby. I wish I never killed it. I love it. I love it more than me. I should just do it... I should.

∞

Group Therapy Session

Therapist: "So... you say you heard a voice speak to you last night Mariah?"

Me: "Yes."

Therapist: "What did the voice say?"

Me: "He said, 'You are worthless' his voice was cold and low like a monster."

Therapist: "He?"

Me: "Yes, it was Satan."

Therapist: "Satan? ... Ok. I find it interesting that it was a male voice."

Me: "Why? I told you who it was."

Therapist: "Well... let's not assume that Satan talks to us."

Me: "Why not? Don't you know who is talking to you when you hear voices?"

Therapist: "I don't hear voices, Mariah. Do you think it might be possible that Satan was just in your head?"

Me: "NO. He was in my room."

Therapist: "You saw him?"

Me: "I didn't have to see him, but I felt him, I heard his voice outside of my head... he was in my room. He was right next to me, breathing on me. I know that I know that I know it was him."

Therapist: "I think we should try to look into why a male voice was speaking to you last night saying you were worthless. Did he say anything else to you?"

Other group members blankly look past me as I speak like they are watching TV.

Me: "Yes. He said I was going to be unsuccessful and fail in everything I do; including my pursuit to get better. He told me I was a whore who deserved to be burned and tortured. He told me God wasn't going to help me."

Therapist: "Did a man ever say something similar to this in your life?"

Me: "Sure- when I was using and scheming- all the time. But it wasn't a 'voice from the past' it was Satan who was speaking to me."

Therapist: (stares into my eyes... tries to search my soul.)

Me: (I stare back. I know what I know. Go ahead and search me.)

One of the patients glares at me and smirks.

Therapist: "I'm going to talk with your psychiatrist. Let's see if we can't increase the milligrams on your meds, Ok?"

Me: Thinking to myself, 'Sure... fill me with more chemicals. Seems to be working- doesn't it?'

flashbacks

To the one who is victorious, I will give the right to eat from the tree of life, which is in the paradise of God.

∞Revelation 2:7∞

The following entries are of various memories of my life as an addict that would come crashing into my mind unexpectedly. As these memories came; I would write...

Fiend

The sidewalk was frigid and frosted and I was sitting there, holding my knees, watching the steam flow out of my mouth.

I had just left the apartment that I was crashing in, where the old man that lived there, pimped me out.

I left that apartment to go to a different apartment where there would be money and more drugs.

But I ended up getting kicked out of this place, where I was about to get money for dancing for a small group of men.

I was thrown out because I saw this guy had a bag of crack and I wanted it- before I did the deed.

So I went after it, trying to grab it from his harsh hands.

There were about three guys holding me down and I was kicking and screaming, yelling at them to give me the crack.

"Give it to me! Why are you flashing it in front of my face but you won't give it to me?! I need that crack!"

"You have lost your mind, girl. We don't want no crazies up in here. Now- GET OUT!"

I was a baby that was crack addicted and crying and shaking because the drug was no longer in my body. And all I knew at that moment was that I needed it.

Crying and screaming like a newborn withdrawing from crack.

They threw me out of the apartment where I was left in the emptiness of the night... the sidewalk was cold and dirty and I was sitting there, holding my knees.

Thrown like a ragdoll.

A car pulled up, a green minivan. He pulled over and motioned for me to get in the van.

I did. It was cold out.

He told me he was going to drive to get me money and cocaine, but first I had to do what he wanted.

One part of me knew that wasn't true- I knew he wasn't going to come back just to give me drugs and money after I did what he wanted.

But the other part of me; the worthless, dirty, drug addicted newborn, fiend - *she* - thought that it didn't sound like that bad of an idea.

And someone like me deserved to be treated like that.

The evil won and he never came back to give me the drugs or money that I shamefully "earned."

∞

Middle School Halls

I was running through the hallways of my middle school. One of my friends was chasing me. I had just cut my arms with something, I don't remember with what. I was in one of my manic psychotic episodes... where my world turned into a sick reality of a bad dream- that was inescapable.

I was drowning in the dream- only the dream was really happening... I drowned in fear and angst.

So I yelled and screamed through the hallways... completely gone... running and I ran, and ran and ran.

I couldn't breathe and the cement was hard under my feet. The cement pounded up my body but I kept running away from myself.

I wanted to just jump out of my body and into the abyss. All my life I just wanted to jump out of my soul.

∞

Engine Gas Suicide Attempt

I was pulled out of my bed in the middle of the night by some force. I walked down the stairs and got my mom's car keys. I opened the door to the garage and got inside her car.

As I put the key in the ignition, I rolled down the windows and prepared to die.

The engine started... like a big cough at first, then slowed to a soft growl.

I sat in the car... deeply breathing in the fumes... waiting.

Eventually I got bored because I wasn't dying fast enough, so I turned on the radio. I remember a song I liked was on and I started to think about how fun it would be to dance to that song at our middle school dance that upcoming weekend. I still desired my seventh grade experiences yet was so warped and suicidal at the same time.

My memory blurs as I try to remember exactly how I got back upstairs and into my bed. But that's where I found myself in the morning- safely in bed.

∞

Razor Suicide Attempt

Raging music blasted in my room. I had purple carpet and loud, purple striped wallpaper. I glared in the mirror at the ugly, distorted image. My heart felt like it was going to leap out of my chest. My anxiety heightened. My 15 year old body burned with anger.

Something took over my whole being as I began to be bothered by the thoughts that yelled in my head;

"Ugh! I'm so ugly!" I thought, full of rage.

"I am done. Get me out!"

I grabbed a razor blade that I saved for such a time as this... and I sought some relief. I sliced my arm. It wasn't enough. I sliced again, this time deeper...

... finally some peace.

I remember feeling at ease, but then getting scared because I cut so deep and the blood wasn't stopping and I wasn't dead yet. I thought maybe I would end up like one of those people who have to get their arm amputated because they did stupid things like this.

I put a Kleenex on my arm and was extremely frustrated that I was still trapped. The Kleenex needed to be replaced and it hurt badly. I hastily thought that maybe I should go get my mom, but I didn't want to tell her what I had done.

I just wanted to stay in my room and curl up and die and stop hurting. I just wanted to stop hurting, stop hurting, stop hurting.

In the morning I woke up with the Kleenex stuck in my arm. I started to pull it out and it became hot with pain. Pieces of Kleenex remained in my wound and I left it in there and bandaged up the evidence.

My soul wept and sorrow ate me alive.

I just wanted it to stop hurting.

∞

Drunk Driving and Overdose Suicide Attempt

I had just gotten arrested- again. This time it was my second Driving While Intoxicated charge. I just crashed my car into a ditch after leaving a party. I remember steering my car right into the ditch like some force took over me and took control of my arms. It was late at night.

I fumbled out of the car, *"I'm not dead?"*

The whole front end of my car was totaled. There was another car that pulled over to see if I was okay. I was weeping and crying. I was so sad. They must have called the police... I fought the cop. I fought him hard. I was violent with rage. He had to shove my face into the ground; I remember the taste of dirt and him yelling at me to, *"Shut up! Stop fighting!"*

Eventually I was in the back of an ambulance- fighting with them too. They took my Blood Alcohol Content and it was well over point two- a deadly high level for a petite girl like me. I was carted off to the emergency psych ward. Familiar ground.

I always knew how to get out of the psych ward- by convincing them I wasn't going to kill myself and that it was the alcohol or drug that made me attempt.

The very next night that I was released from the hospital I bought a bottle of Tylenol PM and two candles. I went into my room after spending the afternoon smoking blunt after blunt of marijuana. I didn't write a note; although it crossed my mind that maybe I should let my family know why I was killing myself. But I didn't. They were better off without me.

I asked God, *"Please take me soul."*

I lay on my bed and swallowed the whole bottle of Tylenol PM. I forgot to light the candles that I bought for a calm ambiance to bring me into death's arms.

My mom came down to my room at about 2am. She said she had a 'feeling.' She said I was standing there with my pants wet (I had urinated myself).

I think it's interesting that I was standing... someone stood me up so I wouldn't choke on my vomit- I realize now it could only have been Jesus.

She took me upstairs and I started tripping out and talking to people that weren't there, hearing things and projectile vomiting. Apparently I was violently ill for a long time. My mom and dad had to take care of me like I was a baby. Urinating and vomiting on myself all over the place... yes, it's glamorous being a suicidal addict.

I finally came to consciousness days later and my mom was sitting right next to me on my bed. I remember asking her, *"I didn't die?"*

"No sweetheart, you didn't. You're alive."

∞

Choking Suicide Attempt

I was working at a nursing home, where my 95 year old Nana lived. I was a very hard worker- high or not high. As I was helping one of the elderly into their shower, I noticed she had her medication in the dresser drawer. It began to eat me alive... knowing there were narcotics in my reach. The addiction burned inside me. It did not matter who, what or where I was. I just needed to be fed.

The next night while working and coming off as seemingly pleasant while doing my C.N.A. (certified nurse assistant) job- I plotted how to get those pills.

I went into her room when she wasn't there... maybe she was at Bingo Night.

There was a camera in her room, so I unplugged it, but stupidly I showed my face before I got it unplugged. I shook nervously as I took the key she used to lock up that drawer and boldly shoved the key into the hole. I twisted it- opened the drawer- but the key broke inside of the hole, "*Oh no!*" I thought.

I shook more intensely as the longing for those pills overtook my whole being. All that I was, all that I existed for was to be a nervous, shaking heroin addict.

I quickly got the bottles opened and at first dumped a whole bunch into my hand, but then thought it might be too obvious so I put some back. Then I tried to tidy up the mess I made and left the broken key in the hole. I ate some pills and my insides finally settled down a bit.

I felt awful; a dirty, scheming, lying, manipulating, useless drug addict. Addiction always trumped any moral fiber I had inside of my heart. My heart was consumed by the demonic forces of addiction. My body was a slave to heroin, pills, cocaine and any substance to numb me.

The next night at work a State Trooper showed up. I remember getting paged to the lobby, *"Oh man that's it... they know."*

I timidly walked into the office.

"Are you Mariah Tramonto?" asked the State Trooper.

"Yes..." No sense lying now.

The cop was holding a VHS tape in his hands, "Please sit down, I need to ask you some questions."

I wanted to bolt. It took all I had within me to sit down on the hard, plastic chair.

"Mariah we can either do this the hard way or the easy way. Now you either cooperate by telling me the truth, or you lie and we can be here all night."

I started rocking in my chair, feeling like my soul just shattered. There was a struggle going on inside of me. I was fighting the demons. They whispered in my ear, "*You're nothing but a drug- addicted whore who steals from the home where your Nana lives. You are going to BURN in hell."* They tormented me.

I took the lanyard around my neck that held the C.N.A. credentials that I was so proud of- and I firmly tightened it around my neck and squeezed with all I had; harder and harder as I attempted to choke myself to death.

The cop stopped me. He shook his head and said, "Stop doing that. What's wrong with you? You have more serious problems than just addiction young lady, you need help."

"I'm sorry. I'm sorry. I just want to die," I blurted as I began crying.

I didn't want to lie, but I didn't want to tell the truth. I was always so tired of explaining myself. But I knew I was found out so I just had to tell him the reality of my desire to die.

Finally, the interrogation was over and he escorted me to the cop car in handcuffs. And off I went to the psych ward- again.

Another Mental Hygiene Arrest, another crime, another worthless drug addict, taking up the State's time and money. The next day I was released out of the psych ward and went to pick up my last paycheck. Immediately I went into the City of Rochester and bought heroin. And then my Nana died 2 weeks later.

∞

Too Tired to Attempt

I walked into the hospital- willingly this time. I dragged myself in from off the street from a long run with the demons. It was a point in my addiction where I knew I had exhausted every other option; a point where I came to a calm acceptance of death. I wasn't high and I wasn't insane at this particular moment. I was just waiting to be done living.

I came up to the emergency room and carried my backpack full of dirty socks, underwear, a hair brush, a couple pairs of sweatpants and a few t-shirts that were stained with blood by the elbows where I shot up. I also had just ingested the last of the heroin I had and swallowed the last of the Xanax too. It barely scratched the surface and it definitely wasn't enough to kill me, unfortunately.

"Hi. I need to be put away," I stated as I walked into the hospital and up to the check-in desk.

"Okay. What's wrong? How can I help you?" asked the receptionist.

"I'm going to kill myself," I replied.

She looked frightened, grabbed a clipboard and pen and told me to fill out the paperwork and to hang on until she could get me up to the psych ward. I remember her soft, brown eyes. She was spooked.

At this time in my life I was homeless-surviving all over the place. I remember just wanting a place to rest. So at this time, it was more that I needed shelter than that I was actually having another manic episode of a suicide attempt. Sometimes I just didn't have the energy to execute the plan in my head. I was so tired on this day.

I got upstairs and was comforted by the fact that I received complimentary toiletries and clean towels. I felt safe in the psych ward. Safe and clean once I showered the blood stains away and washed my hair of the cigarette and weed smell.

I was grateful to have a bed and a pillow. I didn't have to do anything to sleep there. I just had to tell the doctors how much I was hurting and then I was allowed to stay at the hospital. Everywhere else I had to do things to sleep somewhere. I had to sell myself or exchange drugs or money. At the hospital I could just rest my body- even though in my mind there was a raging battlefield.

They would give me lots of medications that made me sleep all day and night. Finally, some sleep.

∞

the walter hoving home

Shake off your dust; rise UP, sit enthroned, Jerusalem. Free yourself from the chains on your neck, Daughter Zion, now a captive. For this is what the Lord says: "You were sold for nothing, and without money you will be redeemed."

∞Isaiah 52:2-3∞

The following entries are written during my stay at this home... when I gave up trying to get well with human effort and fully accepted God's love and grace to heal me from the inside out.

Today is the first day of the rest of my life. I really feel like this is my chance... my one shot to do good and to be the person I was meant to be. Even my big brother sent me a letter with encouragement and said that we all make mistakes. I feel almost normal! I need to share my story, I need to help others. I'm so hopeful right now. *Thank You God for today.*

∞

Back from church and it was a lot of fun actually. It seemed to soothe me... I felt at home and felt loved and safe. It put me in such a good mood. Maybe my past doesn't matter to God... maybe He really has been there for me and really does want me to live a healthy, happy and full life.

God, please help me to read the Bible. I pray that when I read it, I am not confused but that I would stand in awe of You. I pray that You keep all of us safe from evil and that You protect and guide us all in the Holy Spirit. I pray for each of the girls here in this home, that You would show them a new way of life and that we don't have to live like we were living. Thank You, Jesus.

∞

Definitely a bad morning... going on two hours of sleep and a wicked migraine has been my companion. The associate director let me take off from the learning center this morning. I just need to rest my eyes. I didn't fall asleep but I did rest and cried for the first time in a while. I'm just so frustrated as to why I have to be in pain every day. I know I deserve it, but it's just so overwhelming. Excedrin doesn't even work anymore. I need a break from meds I think. I need pictures of my family... *Dear God, I am so sorry for not being the best child in the world. But I want to do something about it. I want to make a change for You. I want to be a role model and put all my trust in You. Please hear my prayer... and deliver me from evil. I know with You all things are possible. Also, please help me to get the sleep I need in order to function. Thank You for today. Please help me to trust You fully.*

∞

It's 3am and I'm awake like always. I'm hungry but at least my head feels better. I'd rather have no sleep than a migraine all day. I think I'm still withdrawing because I need to rock my legs a lot and I get goose bumps all the time. It's been about 2 months now since being on Methadone. Some of my veins are coming back slowly but surely. I have a bad cough and feel sick though... when will I start to feel better?

∞

So today has been physically draining. We had to shovel wet dirt and clay for 4 hours! That was manual labor- for men! It's all good though, I love exercise. At one point Kacey was saying, "I can't do this anymore." So I had her stop and breathe and I talked her out of quitting. She's 44 years old and keeping up like a pro! Earlier today I went to the chapel by myself and prayed. My first time doing that... it was nice and I felt very safe. Maybe I'll do that every night. I asked God if He could hear me. No answer. I didn't expect one anyway. But maybe one day He'll reply in some way I can understand. *God, please let me rest well tonight. Let my true self come out and be a good example to others. Give me strength and the will to not throw up my food. Thank You for all the trials I am going through. Thank You so much. I love You.*

∞

Today I'm not feeling it at all. I don't want to be here- but I don't want to be there either. I don't know what's wrong with me and I hate not knowing how to fix it. I don't like the fact that I have no control over my feelings and emotions. I don't like not being in control... I', scared I'm gonna snap and kill someone. I can't control my anger and when I feel afraid I don't know any other way to deal with my rage other than flipping out and snapping. Why can't I just be happy and hear God speak all the time? I'm depressed and I'm sad and I don't know what to do. I'm not used to feeling any of this stuff... it's weird and I'm not used to it. I really feel like the psych ward might be the only place I feel safe and sound- on lots of medicine and sleeping pills and just zoning out and not thinking or feeling *anything*. I don't want to feel at all! But I asked God for it, I asked to feel... so I better appreciate it.

∞

Dear Lord, I'm praying for Your protection and forgiveness. I know what I've done in life was terribly wrong and I promise to never do stuff like that again, ever! I feel like such a dirty person and I know that's not who I am. Why can't I see the light? Why can't I see the good in me? Why do I always focus on the bad and keep falling backwards? I'm desperately asking for Your help and to teach me the way to righteousness. I would give anything to just travel through time past all this huge mess I made for myself. When I do bad things, it's like my conscience isn't there and isn't telling me "no." I need help to start making the right decisions now. Please forgive me, Lord, and show me the way. Amen.

∞

I feel weird because I don't have an attitude about being here. I'm actually grateful to be here, but everyone else always says they are miserable here and just complains. OH, my ears, please! It could be SO much worse, people. I mean, I am miserable with headaches and insomnia but I still smile through it. I feel like there's hope for everyone if they just try to seek out God. I really think prayer is so powerful now. I am finding it helps to overcome a lot! I am so thankful there aren't many words to express it. I feel like I'm almost ready to deal with some things... and I think maybe I already am. *Thank You, Jesus.*

∞

Last night was rough. I had real bad anxiety and couldn't sleep. I was up every hour and had to rock myself. Then Jess who sleeps next door was snoring so loud! I wanted to punch the wall and scream. But I handled it well, I think, by not punching anything...

∞

I really need Your help, please, I need You to help me. I need to feel and to heal. I don't think I have yet... I don't even think I've opened any of those old doors yet. Please help me with rest too, God. I'm so tired and when I wake up in the night I can't get back to sleep. I pray for everyone else who's suffering, that You would hug them and help them through. I pray that You would give me emotions today..., please help me get stuff out.

∞

Goodbye Satan,

You will not consume me anymore. I'm angry, I'm so angry I let you consume me, control me, hurt me and lie to me. You told me I was worthless. You told me to give up... and I listened. Well now it's time to say GOODBYE and GOOD RIDDENS. I am *so* done with you.

∞

I feel I don't have peace and I want it bad. I want God to come into my heart and change my thinking. I want to live today. I *have* to be grateful even though I'm only crawling towards God. I *have* to be grateful because at least I'm not where I was yesterday. I *have* to be grateful I have all my fingers and toes and I have a brain that works... kind of, anyway. I'm grateful that my family still loves me even though I've done so many awful things. I'm grateful that God loves me so much that I'm actually starting to believe He really does want me and I don't have to prove myself to Him. Today I'm grateful because I'm not sticking myself with dirty needles, not fiending for more, not selling my body and I'm not purposely trying to die. I'm so grateful that I have yet another chance to be who I was meant to be. I am grateful I'm no longer strapped to a hospital bed in the psych ward and that I'm not a bloody, screaming mess. I *have* to be grateful because if I'm not then I'm telling God that all He's done for me doesn't matter. I still have a hard time believing that God loves me unconditionally and that I don't have to jump through hoops to get to Him. All I have to do is pray and seek Him. And most importantly, I think, is to be grateful-whatever the circumstance.

∞

Pretty sure I am going backwards... I feel like crying but I can't. I'm so full cuz I stuffed my face and I dunno why I keep wanting to barf- I haven't in so many years. I feel like I'm regressing... and it's scary. I'm trying not to think about these things but it's so hard. It's *so hard-* why? Why now? Why, when I'm finally off all drugs? It's like I can never just have peace of mind. *Never.* Always, there has to be something wrong and it's really frustrating me. I just want answers- *now.* I miss my dad and mom. I just feel I need some rest. I just went to the chapel and sat with God- I think. I feel really depressed all of a sudden and nauseous. My period still hasn't come yet and I'm getting nervous about it. I dunno what to think anymore. I'm confused and exhausted and bitten by bedbugs and no drugs and no sex and worry and lots of guilt and shame and sadness tonight.

∞

Please God, give me rest. I need to ask You a very big question... could You rid me of my obsessions and compulsions? My addiction is too powerful for me to handle and I need Your help, Lord. Please come into my life and take control- I'm losing it. Thank You for saving my life so far and for listening to me tonight.

∞

Lately I have been really struggling with my self-image. Ever since I began ballet when I was six years old, I started to scan and analyze my body way too much. I compared my body to other girls' and I thought I should slim down. I have never been overweight; just have thought so in my mind. I learned how to throw up my food when I was about 13. I even taught other girls how to do it. My obsession with weight comes and goes nowadays and the thought of having extra fat on my body bothers me so much. It's a distraction from growing closer to God, I know it is. I just try really hard to keep scriptures going in my head and flowing out of my mouth all day. This too will pass... just something I'm struggling with today.

∞

Tonight after dinner I threw up my food for the first time in six years. I'm just having a lot of emotions go through me right now and I dunno how to deal with it all! I wanna use real bad, I wanna stick a needle in and see the blood draw back. I wanna feel the rush, but most of all... I just wanna fly away.

∞

What is wrong with me? A better question would be; what is right with me? Cuz right now I feel like I'm suspended and hanging on a weak branch on a dead tree that's loosely planted on the edge of a rocky cliff. I'm anticipating the fall and I don't want it to come. I wanna hang onto that branch and just keep looking up. I wanna be happy- not pretend happy. People think I'm carefree, strong, sweet, loving and caring. And maybe I am- but why can't I believe that? Why do I dwell on everything that's wrong? My obsessions are obsessed with obsessing my mind. Inside my head is an army of lies and they're so good at lying- that I believe them. I am brainwashed by people, doctors, counselors, experiences, authorities. There are about one hundred voices in my head and each one tells me something different. I've never been so confused, conflicted and trapped inside myself. My bulimia is worse, I am thinking of killing myself again, I wanna slice my wrists, I wanna cry and I can't. I wanna run away and use my drugs... I wanna get out all the things I've done. I need to get them out but I'm crippled. So if I'm crippled, how then can I let go of that branch?

∞

God,

Please, please, please save me. I'm so sorry, I'm so sorry. Please forgive me.

∞

Well today was interesting. We had a prophetic, paralyzed pastor come to our chapel service and anointed almost all of us with oil. He was handicapped and I remember laughing at him during the service as he was preaching because he kept hobbling back and forth and speaking in a loud manner. After his message he gave an altar call. I went up hesitatingly and knelt in the corner by the altar and I said to God internally, *"God- if You are real then tell that pastor to pray for me right now."* It wasn't 5 seconds later that the pastor turned around sharply; leaving the dozens of other girls lined up to be prayed for by him that he pointed at me; boldly telling me to, *"Get up."*

I stared at him in wonder and obeyed his directive. He told me that I was hurting. He said that I'm not ready to help others yet. He asked what I needed prayer for and I said my headaches. So he prayed for me. It felt good. He also told me not to leave here and that I'd been thinking about it- that it's only the Devil trying to get me back.

I really pray that God will open me up like a book and use me to help others. But first, I want Him to heal me. I know I am skeptical of what happened today- how he seemed to know things about me- but I feel strong peace also.

∞

God keeps answering my prayers. I am so thankful! I was starting to think I couldn't cry or grieve- and I can! I went to the chapel again by myself and started to open up to God about my abortion I had when I was seventeen. I began pouring my heart out to Him... and He was faithful to answer me. He showed me a vision of His huge hand holding my baby and that He is taking care of my baby for me. *Thank You, Jesus! It is my joy to serve You. I worship You. You spoke to me and You assured me that my baby is with You and that he's being taken care of and that he's waiting for me until I get there! I'm finally at peace with what I've done and accept Your love and forgiveness.*

∞

Today was a good day. I was up since 2:50am but I kept praying and asking for help all day.

∞

Thank You God for my salvation. I pray for all the girls here, especially the young ones... I see myself in them and I feel their despair and share in their pain.

∞

You know when you feel like you can't go on anymore? That's how I feel today. I'm really scared that me being off of drugs and psych meds is just a dream, it's too good to be true. Can I really stay away from that life forever? All I have to do is ask God for help? Is there no stipulation or condition to God's love? I've had to be strong for so long that I feel so uncomfortable being weak... but when I am weak then I am strong. I'm scared that the next I use will be my last and my counselor used to say that to me all the time, she'd say, "Mariah, you use to *die*- not to get high." Boy, was she was right.

∞

Today is just one of those days where I don't know if I can make it. I feel like I need to cry all the time, day and night. But I am physically unable. I think I've become so desensitized that my body doesn't know how to feel certain things. I struggle so deeply with self-hate. I hate myself because I'm never good enough, I can never do anything good enough and I always feel like people don't understand me because I can't make sense when I try to explain my feelings.

∞

Father please take away the memories of when I was in prostitution. This morning I've been getting physically sick thinking about the stuff I did. Heal my Lord, take it from me. I praise You and thank You... forgive me.

∞

God thank You for this day. I pray for Your strength today. I pray for Your love to overflow in me. Please give me the courage to face my trials. Please give me patience. Please continue to show me things. Continue to bless my mind and bless what comes out of my soul. Please remain in me today. I pray for rest and peace. Please allow me to sleep and awake refreshed so I can continue on in Your strength. I pray for the girls here, that You would show Yourself to them, please help them with all that they are struggling with. Thank You.

∞

Thank You for setting me free. I love You, Jesus. I am Yours.

∞

Dear Father thank You for a new day. Thank You that I'm sober and that I don't have to take a million meds for my brain. Thank You that You've been giving me a wonderful sleep lately. Thank You that You've moved me to tears. Thank You that I'm not a robot and that I have real feelings.

∞

I am sharing with the girls in the home today something I have been learning. Every month or so you are chosen to do a "share." This means that we have to put together like a 5 minute sermon of stuff we've been learning or things that God is showing us. I really like sharing! Lately I've been thinking about this parable in Matthew 13:24-30:

"The kingdom of heaven is like a man who sowed good seed in his field. But while everyone was sleeping, his enemy came and sowed weeds among the wheat, and went away. When the wheat sprouted and formed heads, then the weeds also appeared.

The owner's servants came to him and said, 'Sir, didn't you sow good seed in your field? Where then did the weeds come from?'

'An enemy did this,' he replied.

The servants asked him, 'Do you want us to go and pull them up?'

'No,' he answered, 'because while you are pulling the weeds, you may root up the wheat with them. Let both grow together until the harvest. At that time I will tell the harvesters: First collect the weeds and tie them in bundles to be burned; then gather the wheat and bring it into my barn.'"

I thought it interesting that God would allow evil to be grown with good. He allows bad things to happen to us because we wouldn't fully develop without them. These things happen to test and forge our character. He knows they are ultimately used for our good.

The other day while I was working with the maintenance team, I observed this analogy of weeds unfold before my eyes. I was pulling weeds on the front lawn of one of our staff members' homes and hit a real firm one and was pulling with all my might! I spent all afternoon trying to figure out how I could get it out of the ground. I finally realized I was trying to pull out a root of a beautiful bush and not a weed! How smart am I?! Well, I likened this experience to our spiritual lives and thought that when we do things in our own strength and knowledge we get nowhere. I was trying to pull up a weed which was actually a root and it was not supposed to come out of the ground! The root is good and absolutely necessary to the growth of the plant. The root is vital.

Our faith (roots) should be so firmly planted in the Word of God that no enemy can tear it away from us. We need to let the weeds and the wheat grow together. Once the weed has developed that character in us *He will* pull it out.

∞

God please make me cry

I looked and saw all the oppression that was taking place under the sun: I saw the tears of the oppressed- and they have no comforter. And I declared that the dead, who had already died, are happier than the living, who are still alive. But better than both is the one who has never been born, who has not seen the evil that is done under the sun.

∞Ecclesiastes 4:1-3∞

The following entries are written during a time of contemplative searching...

As it turns out, I'm not a robot. A few months ago my ability to cry was only in the Spirit. I would cry at how grateful I was to be saved, but I could not cry in the natural.

I prayed for tears for a whole year. Yesterday, I finally let my guard down and people saw me cry... I cried because I was sad- not because I was full of joy.

God knew I needed a while to stabilize and not get overwhelmed with my suppressed emotions. Now He is reaching into my innermost being and giving me the gift of emotion.

Tears are okay after all... there's nothing to be afraid of when you're ready to feel.

∞

I'm sure this is weird to some people that a person would keep writing about experiencing tears... but I didn't cry for a very long time. So it is foreign for me to have this gift of crying.

I have a memory of crying in my addiction. I would cry when the drug dealers weren't on the street and I needed a hit. I would cry when I got beat for my money, or sold a fake bag. I cried when I had to take the bus in the winter for two hours to buy five dollars' worth of coke and wait around for the dealer to re-up and then another two hours to get home and then it was gone.

And then I was alone once again in my obsessively, distorted, sick mind.

I cried when I was done selling myself one time and when I was coming down a flight of stairs from leaving his apartment and I tripped and fell. And I cried, *"Stupid heels."*

At that point I sought to go numb by swallowing a fistful of my psych meds and painfully wait to stop feeling.

One hundred and ten milligrams of liquid methadone, ten milligrams of Xanax, four milligrams of Klonopin, and two blunts of weed, a bottle of charcoal tasting vodka, three bundles of heroin, five Ambien, a handful of my prescription meds and thirty dollars' worth of cocaine- a day. It didn't numb me enough.

No amount of drugs could stop the pounding pain in my black heart.

I cried and shook today as I worshipped and praised God. I just want more of Him.

∞

You know that feeling... it's indescribable, inexpressible and almost unbearable because you might just explode.

It's fire, it's fuel, it's food.

It is overwhelming when God gives you His presence. I had to stop right in the doorway and cry to God my expression of thankfulness.

I started praising Him and I fell to my knees. When I don't know how to tell God how I feel- I just fall to my knees and humbly accept His burning love for me.

∞

refiner's fire

But He said to me, "My grace is sufficient for you, for my power is made perfect in weakness." Therefore I will boast all the more gladly about my weaknesses, so that Christ's power may rest on me. That is why, for Christ's sake, I delight in weaknesses, in insults, in hardships, in persecutions, in difficulties. For when I am weak, then I am strong.

∞2 Corinthians 12:9-10∞

The following is written around the same time as experiencing an immense amount of emotions and tears. There was so much that needed to be purged from my soul.

The last several months I have been in the desert. Meaning; I have not felt or heard from God directly. To me, the desert is a wilderness of confusion and suffering without the presence of God. I do not like the desert and sometimes I feel like I may be stuck there.

But I know I have freedom! And I hold onto remembering what God has done for me.

I recently prayed and broke through the bondages of soul ties from my past. I truly am set free from the souls that I have regretfully tied my soul with. It was so hard to write the list of people I have been with, but I did it because I want to be obedient and I desperately want to be free in Jesus.

Once you have been through the fire of hell, there is nothing more important or satisfying than to find peace in resting under the shadow of the Almighty. There is *nothing* more important to me than my relationship with Jesus.

∞

While I am on this journey of affliction that God is bringing me through, I will maintain an attitude of gratitude by remembering how much worse I could be. I will remember through my fire of doubt, that Jesus had gone through being crucified and killed- for me. I will remember God's grace and that He will pull me out at just the right time, because it will be *His* time. And I will continue to praise the mighty name of Jesus Christ.

∞

Although I am suffering in my faith- I have to keep looking towards the cross. I know deep within my very being that there is more to life than what we live each day on earth.

Doubt tries to play games with my mind and pull me back under and into the abyss.

But I hold on tight to my Refuge and Fortress. I hold tight to the promises in the Word and the promises God has spoken to me. I hold tight to my testimony- that I have been set free from drug addiction, prostitution, mental illnesses, eating disorders, self-mutilation and so much more. I overcome by speaking and remembering what God has done for me.

I overcome by covering myself with the blood of Jesus.

∞

This scripture is giving me what I need today...

1 Peter 1:6-7

In all this you greatly rejoice, though now for a little while you may have had to suffer grief in all kinds of trials. These have come so that your faith- of greater worth than gold, which perishes even though refined by fire- may be proved genuine and may result in praise, glory and honor when Jesus Christ is revealed.

∞

Something that an addict grieves over is their lifestyle. It's hard to comprehend why someone would grieve the chaotic life of an addict, of being homeless and barely surviving. Every other time I've tried getting sober, it was with the worlds so-called "help" and it left me empty... every time. The therapy and medications are endless.

Lamentations 3:19

The thought of my suffering and homelessness is bitter beyond words. I will never forget this awful time, as I grieve over my loss.

It is true, that the addict feels a significant and powerful loss when the drugs and lifestyle are absent. It's a deep sense of hollowness and sadness... like a child lost in the grocery store.

The chasing, the needles, the hustle, the buying and selling, the running from cops, the arrests, the fingerprints, the prostituting, blacking out, lying and stealing. The *screaming*. The doctors telling you they don't know how you could come out of this alive- except that it could only be a miracle.

∞

One of my many thorns in the flesh is that I get migraines. I've had them since I was ten years old. I throw up and everything.

When I was taking every pill known-to-man, I couldn't really feel the pain. Now, without the pill habit it's very obvious when I'm hurting physically.

When I used to have bouts of sobriety, one of the reasons the drugs would call me back would be to calm the pain in my body- the pain without drugs and the pain in my head.

The pain of who I had become was too much to handle. The dirty drug addict in my past was constantly hounding me to come back, like a pig returning to its vomit.

Although these flashbacks still arise- they don't have to taunt me anymore because I finally accepted forgiveness. The love of Jesus makes all things new. Jesus has given me the way out.

I don't have to live in fear or guilt anymore. Paranoia is something that Jesus does not give me.

So when I am in pain I remember how much worse my pain used to be and then I thank my God and continue on the path.

∞

I am thinking about the scripture I just read in Isaiah 40:31 (NLT), it says- *But those who trust in the Lord will find new strength. They will soar high on wings like eagles.*

They will run and not grow weary. They will walk and not faint.

This made me think about perseverance. In my old dance studio there was a poster up on the brick wall that said *perseverance* and it had a picture of a ballerina in her point shoes on it.

I remember looking up at that poster when attempting to do hard ballet moves, as I bit my lip wiped the sweat off my face and I wondered what exactly that word meant.

When you're falling into the pit and not seeing anything but black emptiness surrounding you, it is hard to press on.

What exactly are you pressing for?

If you see no good in your life except for a needle full of heroin and hopefully a cigarette to bum from someone- *then what is it that you're going to do with your life?*

I wrestled with that question for so long- the big question of why any of us are alive.

It takes a lot of courage to push through the past. Some of our pasts are absolutely terrifying- who would want to deal with it?

Perseverance is when you get to the place where you take responsibility for all the evil you've done and all the evil you've seen and you *do something about it.*

Perseverance is when everybody around you tells you, "You can't get sober, you can't get off those psych meds, you can't even sit still for two seconds without fiending for the next one- look at you- you're disgusting!"

And yet- you keep going.

Perseverance requires patience, determination and willingness to learn the Truth and do things differently no matter what the cost. The Trust (Jesus) tells me, *"I am fearfully and wonderfully made."* He tells me, *"I am more than a conqueror,"* and God says He *"knew me before He formed me in my mother's womb."*

Perseverance is described in the dictionary as; steady persistence in a course of action, especially in spite of difficulties, obstacles, or discouragement.

I think the harder your past was to deal with- the better your future will be if you can make the decision to persist on a positive course of action despite your obstacles. When you have trekked and toiled in the dark night your reward of reaching the Light is just *that much sweeter* than if you have never experienced any pain at all.

∞

Jesus says in Luke 10:18, "I saw Satan fall like lightening from heaven."

I remember when I was in the Walter Hoving Home and I had a vision of Satan and my baby whom I aborted. I was watching a DVD called Healing Abortions in the learning center when all of a sudden I received in my mind, a picture of Satan holding my baby. He was monstrous, pure evil and deceptively grinning at me. I jumped back in my chair and became incredibly frightened.

I began diligently seeking God... asking Him where my child was and how I can I know I am truly forgiven for that and lots of other questions. I thought my baby was in hell with Satan. Did my decision to abort my baby lead him or her to a final resting place with the enemy?

Was my baby crying or scared? Was he hungry? Alive? ...in the arms of Satan?!

I hadn't slept for months when this happened because of serious withdrawal symptoms and during this torturous vision

you can forget about any sleep at all.
Satan was holding my baby and laughing
at me... I was so scared.

But my faith in God increased at this time
because, I asked, how can Satan exist and
not God?

After much time on my knees in battle, the
Lord showed me that He had my baby and
spoke to me gently, yet firmly, saying;
*"Your baby is being taken care of and
loved, and he will be waiting for you when
you get here."*

Then I was able to cry... and cry... and cry.

I cannot wait for the day when I will meet
him, hug and kiss him.

When I was in this spiritual battle it was of utmost importance to remember my authority in Christ by not getting sucked into the lies the enemy was telling me, or this case showing me through a vision.

Jesus tells me that in Luke 10:19, *"I have given you authority to trample on snakes and scorpions and to overcome all the power of the enemy."*

I had every reason to believe Satan... I aborted my child when I was seventeen, I used drugs while I was pregnant, and I was indeed an awful, shameful, evil and selfish person. Wouldn't it make sense that my baby was in hell? And I that I should forever pay for what I did by soon joining him in the fire of endless torture?

Because of the vision I had of Satan holding my baby- I was almost forced to seek God. Either that, or go jump off a high building. I *had* to seek answers... and Truth.

And do you know how good God is? He, in turn, gave me a heavenly vision! It was three days after this horrible vision of Satan that I was laying on my bed that evening. I was thinking about Jesus and what He said to me earlier that day about how He had my baby... I was so thankful and grateful... just lying on a bed a peace. And then! Out of nowhere I receive a vision of Jesus on a white horse. He was coming fast toward Satan... He had a huge blade in His hand, drawn for war. He

got to Satan and slayed him right in half!
Jesus looked angry and full of passion.
Satan's arms were broke by the power of
God and I saw my baby drop from his slimy
hold. Finally, I saw God's strong,
humongous hand reach out and catch my
baby.

Peace. Victory! Rest.

∞

Today I am dealing with bad depression. I
am relating to David in Psalm 143:7
(NLT); *Come quickly, Lord, and answer
me, for my depression deepens. Don't turn
away from me, or I will die.*

I feel like I'm questioning everything. My
calling, my focus, my heart, my work, my

dreams, my suffering, my ministry and even *my faith*.

All of it is being questioned. Season of doubt? Season of sadness? I want out but don't know where to go. I want love, truth and assurance. I'm crying hard and I want to keep crying. I feel like I'm spinning out of control. The invading darkness can be so overwhelming at times. My strength is gone. Fatigue is plaguing me. My counting obsession has increased. Sorrow and tears follow me. My head hurts. My heart hurts... levels of pain pulse through me.

My only anchor is my hope in Jesus. He will keep me from drowning. He will keep me from the vultures. Jesus *will* keep me.

∞

Last night I cried in my bathroom. I cried to God and begged Him to take my life. I have come to the point of spiritual dryness and sorrow. *A place of feeling no presence of God.* I am confused and fearing the loss of my mind again. This slowly crept up on me. I was so full of fire when I first got saved and *felt* the Lord walking with me.

But, lately, I have been feeling abandoned. Then today at church, at The Brooklyn Tabernacle, the pastor said he was praying this morning and received a Word; that God knows the pain I am in and that even though I'm in the valley and cannot feel Him, He *is* there watching me. He said I am going through the refiner's fire to prepare me for travel and life of ministry. I received the words from Jesus that I was intensely longing for. I cried and cried and then went to the altar as he prayed for those of us who came forward in desperation for God.

∞

I feel I might be finally coming out of the desert. I was thinking I lost my anointing, but funny thing about the anointing- it isn't mine to begin with! I feel utterly helpless- like I cannot possibly do anything for God. I believe this is right where God wants me. He's steadying my feet so I can walk this out... But I don't want to *walk-* I want to *run* after Jesus.

∞

dreaming

For God does speak- now one way, now another- though no one perceives it. In a dream, in a vision of the night, when deep sleep falls on people as they slumber in their beds, he may speak in their ears and terrify them with warnings, to turn them from wrongdoing, and keep them from pride, to preserve them from the pit, their lives from perishing by the sword.

∞Job 33:14-18∞

The following are a collection of recorded dreams...

Last night in my sleep I cried. I think I was crying because I didn't want to leave somewhere I felt safe, but it was time to move on.

For more than ten years in my life I would run away from home and live in weird places. Anytime I got almost comfortable or safe in one spot, then it was time to run again. The drugs would call me out into the wilderness and I would be all alone searching for my lost soul.

To always be worried about where I would stay the night was stressful. It was my own fault. I was too weak to fight the addiction and it won every time.

I think that's why I was crying in my sleep... I was experiencing those feelings of constantly trying to find a place to rest my head.

I will give you a new heart and put a new spirit in you; I will remove from you your heart of stone and give you a heart of flesh (Ezekiel 36:26).

God is making it possible for me to feel again, and it's okay to be sad for the lost soul that I was... even if it's crying in my sleep.

∞

The following is a poem I wrote about a bad dream of rats and flies attacking me:

Dreams of disgust that seek to drag me into the deep come only to torment me in my sleep.

The mind, I've tried, to push out the things that creep.

This process though is not easy to complete.

Settling, slowly, softly I wait,

For Jesus my Savior to rescue my unconscious fate.

Rats attack me,

Flies and bees swarm into my space.

It's only natural to think I'm not free,

It's supernatural to believe Jesus is my saving grace.

All along this path of pilgrimage,

I learn to find the way and feel.

Dreams of the past I cannot manage,

Sometimes they still seem so real.

God my hope, my help, my healer,

He alone can protect me from the peace-
stealer.

Jesus my sanity, my rest, my redeemer,

He alone can cleanse my mind of evil.

The Holy Spirit is my comforting hug, the
whisper in my ears,

I pray to ask Him to forgive and to wipe my
tears and He says to me:

*"You are a new creation and your past is
gone along with your sins. These dreams
come straight from hell to torture and scare*

you... Satan is the father of lies and he wants you back. But I WON'T let him have you. Trust in Me, in My Word and remember your deliverance in Christ. The blood of Jesus cleanses you from all unrighteousness. Your past is gone, your past is gone, your past is GONE along with your sins."

∞

I awoke with the resin of a filthy dream dripping inside my mind. I was pregnant. I was contemplating abortion. I was fighting myself and wanted to keep the baby. People around me were all gross. I was surrounded by men from the past. There was sex and torment.

This wouldn't have knocked me down so hard today if I hadn't had an abortion when I was seventeen years old.

In my dream, I was frantic... thoughts racing of how I was going to support the baby and there was no father.

It was just me and a bunch of sex-driven men who drove me around in cars and pulled me in different directions. It was just me surviving the evil that impregnated my soul.

There has been a shadow over me all day of gloomy, gross memories... and the sky is gray today. Even the weather agrees.

∞

Utterly exhausted... I've been running in my sleep all night. Fighting, wrestling and my strength waning. I was screaming and shouting- attempting to break free. I remember red eyes glowing and waiting for me. The fear was overwhelming- I felt so scared.

I knew what I needed to do. I prayed in tongues and yelled His name, "JESUS!" I finally awoke in the middle of the night due to the punching, kicking and yelling...

I made it to the bathroom and kept speaking the blood of Jesus over me... I made it back to bed eventually- trusting God to protect me.

∞

Dreams are important to be aware of because they help the mind process and, in turn, to let go. I also think that just because one believes in God your problems and struggles don't go away. In fact, you *will* have spiritual warfare when you believe in Jesus. I think this is one, out of many, evidences that you belong to Jesus.

Bad memories and flashbacks still occur... to think that life will be without sorrow and pain because I believe in God is the exact opposite of what Jesus says; *"I have told you these things, so that in my you may have peace. In this world you will have trouble. But take heart! I have overcome the world"* (John 16:33).

And He also says, *"Beloved, do not think it strange concerning the fiery trial which is to try you, as though some strange thing happened to you; but rejoice to the extent that you partake in Christ's sufferings, that when His glory is revealed, you may also be glad with exceeding joy"* (1 Peter 4:12-13 NKJV).

Believing in God is about embracing the challenges and sorrows with an attitude of hope and joy. We can be joyful in all circumstances not because of our ability, but because of Jesus Christ's ability to give us peace and joy throughout our many trials.

It is now a matter of what I choose to believe; I can either choose to believe I am worthless and should be in hell because of the evil I've done in life. Or, I can choose to believe that Jesus came to seek and to save the *lost*. There is nothing I can do to make myself a good person- we are all sinners who have fallen short of the glory of God. Not any single person on earth deserves to go to heaven for being "good."

But because of God's everlasting, unwavering and passionate love for us- He made a way. The way is Jesus Christ.

"For God so loved the world that He gave His one and only Son, that whoever believes in Him shall not perish but have eternal life" (John 3:16).

∞

I had another nightmare last night but I won't go into detail because it was just perverted.

During the day my dreams are still with me. Sometimes I have difficulty accepting dreams are just dreams and that it doesn't mean that it's reality.

Dreams come from different sources: our own twisted minds, the enemy, the Holy Spirit and ones I define as random nonsense. The one I had last night had been from demons. They can only get to me in dreams because they know how strong the Lord is in me. They try to sway my thoughts into perversion and lust...

But I'm shouting, "VICTORY!"

When the enemy comes in like a flood, the Spirit of the Lord will lift up a standard against him (Isaiah 59:19 NKJV).

∞

I had a dream last night where God told me I had power! He said in His powerful and frightening voice, **"You now have the power to heal."**

Then He put a symbol on my hand and when I awoke my hand was still burning where He placed the symbol.

Then I prayed that He would use me to heal people.

∞

It was a cold and icy night, dark and frigid. This dream I was in my dad's car with him driving. A certain rush ran through my body, almost as a warning signal. We slid on the pavement, hitting a patch of black ice. We spun very rapidly around and around. My dad gave me a look of fright and concern as he put his arm out in front of me- a fatherly gesture to hold me back, as if to conquer Mother Nature. But fate had us crash into something, not sure what exactly, but we were colliding into something fierce. He was wearing a seatbelt so he suffered very little. I, on the other hand, was not seat-belted. First, my head hit the windshield, then my body followed as I soared out of the vehicle and landed disturbingly disheveled onto the road of the freezing night. I lay on the pavement half awake, waiting for help.

Not sure what this means... I know biological fathers represent God in dreams, so maybe it means that I am in a season of learning to trust my Father in life's biggest storms. And I think being in a car accident represents losing control in a dream... so maybe He is teaching me about letting go of control as well.

∞

In last night's dream, I opened the door to my dad's room and there he sat on his bed. He was intently and adamantly studying the Word of God. He had several scriptures underlined and was repeatedly pointing at the scriptures. He looked at me with a bold face, a face of warning- a face

that said, *"Hurry up and read this Word...*

no time to waste!"

∞

brooklyn teen challenge

For one human being to love another: that is perhaps the most difficult of all our tasks... the work for which all other work is but preparation.

∞Rainer Maria Rilke∞

The following entries are written during my internship and life at Brooklyn Teen Challenge.

A girl that was admitted into our program decided to leave the other day. She was in my office and had that look- that salty sea of sadness drowned out her face. She never became addicted- she was suffered with being mentally ill. Her eyes were glazed over as she stared at my office walls.

"So, you going somewhere safe when you leave here?" I asked.

"Yea, I'll be with my grandma." She replied.

"Okay good. You hungry? I have some trail mix."

"Yea, thanks." She munches quietly as she stares off into never-land.

I looked into her eyes and prayed. I remember that glazed, dazed state of mind. It sucks. It's so numb and empty. The only thing good about being dazed out is that there is no feeling (but I'm learning now that feelings *are* a good thing).

Being dazed and confused is like you're skimming along in life and you watch everything pass you by- friends get married, they get pregnant, they finish college and have successful lives. All of this is happening and you don't even know it until you snap back to reality (if you ever do). And then it's like a whirlwind of events that slap you in the face. You feel guilty for not being present in your loved-ones life- even though you may have been there physically.

When someone is that numbed out they have lost all purpose in their life, you wonder what their purpose even is? Maybe it is to be an encouragement for someone if they come out of it or to give comfort and sympathy to their fellow life-sufferers.

Whatever the reason, I know there is hope. I came out of it. I know it is possible. The only catch is that you have to be desperate enough to want help. You have to be ready to surrender everything over to God. He is faithful to deliver you from the worst of the worst of sadness.

∞

I am sad today... usually I prefer to be alone than with a group of people and having to talk about things that don't matter.

Most of the time, I am by myself reading, praying or contemplating something.

The other day someone wanted to come into my room and watch a movie, but I didn't invite her in. I felt kind of bad about it but I just knew that this person would want to talk about things that are meaningless. I would rather spend time speaking with God about things that have meaning than be involved in mindless chatter. I don't mind being with people but sometimes I just don't have the capacity to listen to empty words. Boy, I hope I'm not sounding rude. I am just trying to be honest and share what's on my heart.

Also, I'm sad today because of bills. I hate that something as stupid as a bill can affect my emotional state. Although, I think it had to do with how the guy on the phone talked to me when I tried to reconcile this debt. He didn't listen to me and probably a young teenager working in the collections office. He gave me a lot of attitude and when I got off the phone with him I cried. Not because of him, really, but because I am trying so hard to get my life back together and I think I'm making good progress but the financial part of it sometimes overwhelms me. I do not even have that much debt! I am grateful that I never owned a credit card. I just have student loans that I used to buy heroin with, and some medical bills. Funny, I am still paying for my past heroin use today...

But Jesus often withdrew to lonely places and prayed (Luke 5:16). This scripture gives me comfort. This is what I do most of the time and it is okay that I am sad today. If I was happy and giddy all the time then I would be placed in the category of people who seem fake- and I am anything but fake.

∞

I have been journaling about my weight issue a lot lately... it's not even an issue; really, I am probably underweight if anything. I used to have an eating disorder but I still worry about my weight sometimes.

I think it's been more on my mind lately because there was a dance audition on Saturday at the Brooklyn Tabernacle and I really wanted to go.

I think back to my dancing days and smile at how the music and movement settled my soul. And then obsession came to destroy my love of dance. I stopped dancing because my eating disorder took over and also because getting wasted with vodka and weed turned into more fun than getting wasted with Mozart and leotards.

When I first started getting clean of everything I struggled a lot with getting my angst out of me. I remember sitting on the toilet with a switchblade and carving the word, 'FAT' on my left thigh. I looked at it and sighed with relief. I was still sick.

So now, thinking about trying out at an audition is giving me some concern about my body. It turned out I had to work at the ministry Saturday anyways... so it looks like I will just keep dancing for Jesus and Jesus only... for now.

∞

Last night I walked into a psych ward to check up on a student we have here in the program. I was real nervous at first and counted things anxiously in my head while I breathed in the sterile hallways I walked in and then the doors slammed and locked shut behind me. The walls were so blank and empty and the mood of those present on the floor was numb. Everyone was a robot; methodically acting out what they knew of their reality. Med time was in order and the patients waited patiently for their fix. They waited patiently for their Tic Tacs in a cup.

There were no smiles. But I smiled at everyone I saw and tried to pull some life from them- but they were all dead inside. How can you smile when you are dead?

I decided to morph with them and allow myself to feel the rhythm of the ward. I fully embraced the feeling. It's about time I started to feel.

During the check-in process I got really anxious... I remembered when they had to check my stuff in- no handles, no plastic, no shampoo or deodorant of your own. No hair ties, no elastic, no normalcy. Just bring your sadness. I was anxious because the flashbacks of suicide jumped in my mind and the remembrance of the mournful nights when all that was left in me was death.

One of the nurses was a believer and I could tell as soon as I saw her. She was a light in the dark. The nurses are ones who bring you back to health and if you are doubly blessed, they nurse you back to spiritual health. I love nurses.

I had not entered a ward since the year two thousand nine; so it took me about an hour to finally begin to loosen up. I began to be at ease with myself. I felt like God was healing some left over brokenness. It was good. I focused on the student and we connected on a deep level, something I haven't had in a while. I had a real understanding with her.

At one point she said, "Miss Mariah, I didn't realize how much we are the same."

I said, "Yup."

We both smiled at our shared perception. Sometimes thoughts fly off into the deep. Sometimes we lose ourselves and it's only Jesus who can bring us back.

∞

Although I am building my foundation in the Lord, I do have moments of doubting God's will for my life. Does He really have my life mapped out as long as I am obedient? Does He really have my best interest at heart? Am I serving where and how I am supposed to be? God, are You going to be there for me?

Sometimes I wonder if I will have enough strength to work in ministry my whole life. So many people need help- and I want to help them all. So many people are confused and sad and need to hear that there is help. I am thankful that I am apart of Teen Challenge and can do that every day. I also know that God will take care of His people, and that I cannot possibly save the whole world.

So much goes along with spreading the Word of God; paperwork, meetings, phone calls, frustrations, assignments from leaders and from God. Courage to speak the truth, disciplining for those who are in the wrong, trusting the wisdom God gave me, and how about the most important thing but also the most taken for granted-*prayer!* Seek first the Kingdom of God then everything will come after that. Personally, I don't have time to be discouraged. Thankfully, I can go to any of my sisters here and ask for prayer. Seeking the Lord is not only *critical* it is a command; it is a truth found in the Word and it is absolutely necessary. Without prayer there is no relationship to Jesus, and with no relationship with Jesus... well fill in the blanks.

This experience working at Teen Challenge is a *far* greater experience than working anywhere else. To be a servant is a privilege and I am so grateful that He has saved me and called me to work here. If He calls you- He *will* equip you!

In Matthew 6:33-34, Jesus says, *"But seek first his kingdom and his righteousness, and all these things will be given to you as well. Therefore do not worry about tomorrow, for tomorrow will worry about itself. Each day has enough trouble of its own."*

∞

explosion of grace

Therefore, I tell you, her many sins have been forgiven- as her great love has shown. But whoever has been forgiven little loves little. Then Jesus said to her, 'Your sins are forgiven.'

∞Luke 7:47∞

The following is a brief collection of reflections on just how amazing God's grace really is.

Morning Dew

In the morning when I first wake up I am so grateful...

There is peace within me and no more worrying about where, when and how to get high.

The morning is now calm, clean, contemplative and full of morning dew (that I now notice).

Instead of being full of fear- the morning is full of quietness. I am so grateful that it is no longer noisy and distressing.

My soul can *rest.*

∞

The Pearl of Great Price

Some people have known me as Don Wilkerson's assistant, some know me as a missionary, others may know me as a Jesus-freak, or as a School of Ministry graduate, and as a Walter Hoving Home graduate. Still others know me as a dancer, a poet, a dreamer, a visionary, a lover of children... or as an "old lady" because I go to bed so early and drink chamomile tea at exactly eight p.m. every night.

But do you know me as an intravenous drug user? A crack addict? A mentally ill, suicidal mess? A prostitute? When I was all of those things, God saw through that ugliness and saw my true worth. His love has so pierced my soul that it is my responsibility to tell others of His redemptive power, His everlasting love... His goodness... His mercy.

There are a lot of new things God is doing in this season within each of us. One of which I believe is for all of us, in that He is trying to communicate in new ways to us His full acceptance of our condition. I think the church as a whole is receiving the same message of complete reliance on the Holy Spirit- that we are nothing but a breath in this life. We need to move out of the way and let God work through us as He so desires. God is trying to tell us we are fully accepted, fully loved, fully cared for. We aren't just loved when we do good things. We aren't just accepted when we act normal and are misbehaving. We are being awakened by the revelation of divine rest and complete peace as we cling to the cross, our Anchor, our Hope and our Salvation.

∞

In Matthew 13:45-46 (NKJV) Jesus says; *"The Kingdom of heaven is like a merchant seeking beautiful pearls, who, when he had found one pearl of great price, he went and sold all that he had and bought it."*

This parable focuses on the Merchant, who is Jesus, and the thing that sticks out so much is that it is Jesus who searches for us. We are the pearls He is looking for. I thought it interesting that God is comparing us to pearls- so I looked up the process of pearl creation. There are mollusks that sit on the bottom of the ocean and when an inevitable intruding agent tries entering/attacking the mollusk, the mollusk immediately produces a chemical to form a hardened substance within itself. As more intruders try to enter the mollusk, more and more chemicals are produced to protect and shield the now forming pearl.

The pearl (me and you) represents a vessel that's been constantly attacked by intruders but has remained under the protection of the mollusk. The pearl transforms from nothing into something beautiful and of great price.

I think that intruding spiritual attacks bring about spiritual beauty when we remain under God's protection and love.

Jesus is using the object of pearls to illustrate our great value. In our flesh, we ask, *"How can someone that's been intruded upon and attacked be worth anything at all? How am I of any value? Doesn't God see how beat up I am, how ugly I really am inside?"*

The answer is no. God does not see our ugliness, our bruises, and our scars from intrusions. When He looks at us, He sees beauty. He does not see our sin. He sees love.

The truth is that Jesus not only died for our sins but He sold everything He had- His life- for the most beaten up of us all. The life of Jesus shows God's love coming down to this earth to save us all. Jesus especially came for the ones who have been so attacked and hated by the world that, in fact, He even calls such as these- beautiful.

In Matthew 9:12-13, Jesus says, *"It is not the healthy who need a doctor, but the sick. But go and learn what this means: 'I desire mercy, not sacrifice.' For I have not come to call the righteous, but sinners."*

We are beautiful pearls found by our Merchant, Jesus. Let us rest today in trusting our Father instead of trusting ourselves. Let us find acceptance in the arms of Jesus. Let us make the choice to walk in our full inheritance today and awaken to the revelation that it is all about Him and His desire is to love us. Will we let Him?

∞

Abortion

Abortion is something you never get over. You may process it, your wounds may heal and you may understand that you are forgiven. But the fact still remains that what you've done is permanent.

When the abortion workers told me they were ready to "terminate the pregnancy," they barely looked me in the eye, but they assured me there was no baby forming in my womb, but that is was "just a bunch of cells."

As a seventeen year old cocaine addict I was too numb and in pain to comprehend the facts.

What I've learned is this; we all make horrible, life-shattering decisions when we are hurting and not walking with God. But, what is so amazing about Jesus is that while we are making these decisions He is stretching out His hands to us and whispering, *"I love you anyway."*

∞

Desires

It is so strange to me... this desire to live a quiet, peaceful life. To have a family; to be a mom? How can I do something that simple? Why do I always choose chaos and busyness? I am split between two desires: One- to live life as a missionary for Jesus. Adventure, saving souls, rescue, changing the world, to live on the brink of death, to expel demons, plant ministries, preach and teach. To live by faith alone. To see and experience miracles, to heal the sick.

Desire number two is to fall madly in love. Get married and have twelve children. To live on a farm in the middle of nowhere, grow food on the land, ride a horse. Wake up early to milk cows? Feed lots of

children. Make love to my husband all day.
Play with my daughter's hair. Love Jesus.
Teach my children to love Jesus.

Two very strong desires, indeed.

∞

a time for everything

There is a time for everything, and a season for every activity under the heavens: a time to weep and a time to laugh, a time to mourn and a time to dance...

∞Ecclesiastes 3:1, 4∞

The following entries are written during times in Africa, dating and engagement, dancing with the Brooklyn Tabernacle Dance Ministry, and finally, leaving Brooklyn Teen Challenge to begin a new chapter in life.

Swaziland

I have been asking God for more faith and ability to believe. The only reason I am saved and am submerged in the Holy Spirit is because I believe! But I want more! Maybe it's my addictive nature that makes me this obsessive about receiving more of God. I don't know, but as long as I'm addicted to Jesus- then what's the harm in that?! Who can be against me?

Today as I fast, I'm praying for an increase in faith and an increase in clarity when studying God's Word. I have one focus in life- and that is to be with Jesus. To learn from Him, to love Him and to serve Him. Of course I have other wants in my life... but I am willing to give them all up if it means making my God happy with what I'm doing with the life He gave me.

I am also fasting for my upcoming trip to Swaziland! Brother Don (my boss, the president of Brooklyn Teen Challenge) is sending me to Swaziland, Africa with Bernie and Cathy Gillott (Global Teen Challenge Evangelism Coordinators).

I am ready! I am being sent-out! What an honor to be used by God in this way. I pray God will open the heavens and show me His face.

∞

First day here in Swaziland... wow,... breathtaking mountains and so many tall trees. I just met the directors of this Teen

Challenge, as well as several beautiful orphans. God spoke to me saying this was His heart- the orphans, the poverty, the suffering and the sad. That's where His heart is.

∞

Yesterday an orphan called me, "Mommy"... broke my heart in a million, messy pieces. I love these kids so much; there are so many of them. So many children- almost all of them are fatherless. I am bursting with gratitude and joy being with them. I can't wait to be with the kids again tomorrow.

∞

It has been a busy few days of editing and filming with Bernie at this Teen Challenge center. I am now looking at the most beautiful mountains and listening to cows moo. It is absolutely wonderful.

This morning I spent time in a village where I learned of the Swazi culture. The witch doctors are very important to the Swazi people. Then I went to the Teen Challenge women's home and shared my testimony. I was so blessed. Some of the girls here have their children living with them. When I walked in, one of the children ran up to me and put his arms up. I am in heaven.

∞

Today we drove up to a dried up river. We saw a lot of sad, hungry and poor children just wandering. There was a man sitting in the middle of the river. I asked our guide what he was doing there. He said he was a Swazi pastor, praying that God would bless the river and make it rain. They had gone a long time without fresh water and there was a lot of sickness among the people. It was heartbreaking to see such poverty and weariness. We prayed also that it would rain and that the river would be full again.

∞

We had awesome prayer time this morning, Jesus was there. I saw Him touch the guy's head next to me and then He touched my head. Then I saw Him touch the guy's heart who was praying. Thank You Jesus for spiritual sight... You are so beautiful.

∞

It rained! It rained! God answered our prayers and the river is full of fresh water! The people can eat and drink again!

∞

Back to Brooklyn

I am so totally drained... memories keep popping up of my time in Swaziland. I am struck by the oppression there. I will never forget that place. I am in love with the children and I have so much respect for Teen Challenge workers all over the world. *Thank You Jesus, I love You so much.*

∞

A Time to Dance

I finally got the courage to take some dance classes in Manhattan! I am feeling so liberated! I'm taking modern and ballet... my two favorites. Oh, the joys of a good jete, pada bouree!

Well... I was in church the other week at the Brooklyn Tabernacle and the dance leader was brought on stage to talk about the dance ministry. I felt a strong pull to talk to her and find out more about it.

I have been coming to this church for a couple years now and every year they have an announcement for the Christmas dance performance and that there will be an audition for dancers and actors. I always want to try-out, but my fear always discouraged me.

Well! Not this time! I talked to Ashley, the dance leader, after that church service and I gave it a shot. It was like seven hours of auditioning... I was so nervous but once they gave us the combination I loved it! And I just danced it. And they accepted me.

I really feel this will be an awesome outlet and something that I can do outside of Teen Challenge.

∞

Courtship

I just ended an online relationship with this guy who seemed spiritual but what I found was that he was a stumbling block sent to distract me and bring me down. I am grateful that I got to know him though, and that I found out what I *don't* want in a man. So for that I am thankful.

My aunt just got ahold of me on Facebook and introduced me to this guy named Zander. She said he is serious about his walk with God and that he is looking for a godly wife. It's funny because I just was earnestly praying that God would bring me my husband soon... hmm, I wonder?

∞

So I just talked to Zander on the phone... ha-ha... he sounds like a nerd. But I really like how different he is. I think he was really nervous... and I love that he wasn't cocky, smooth or slick with his words. Girls- run the other way when you hear a man like that! Zander has never been with a woman, never done drugs, a true servant, a worshipper with a good and pure heart. I can see that. He may be slightly awkward, but who cares?! It really feels like God just straight up answered my prayer... just like that. I have no idea if he is "the one," but what I do know is he is God-sent. Even if it's just for a season, he is here to show me what a true man looks like.

The guy I ended it with emailed me but I didn't respond. And I never will again. He is so lame.

∞

Zander came to see me yesterday. I don't understand it. My brain is going crazy trying to figure out why someone would want to drive all day to see me. I want to just accept this- that it's an answer to prayer, that it's a gift from God but it's so difficult because I don't feel like I deserve someone like this. And I can't help but think there's got to be something wrong with him or something... but I don't see anything wrong. In fact, I had a really nice time with him yesterday. Really, I did! It was healthy, safe, comfortable, appropriate, godly, substantial and fun. I mean- I don't get it. *God- if this is from You then please give me a huge smack in the head... even though You already answered my prayer about sending me a man who is all about You into my life (ASAP). I mean You did that. So now I doubt You? And of course, I have to start thinking there's gotta be something wrong with him for him to just come here. It's too romantic- too much of a fairytale. Guys are really like that? Tell me. I want to know. Love, Your perplexed daughter.*

∞

I had a dream about Z the other night. We were sliding down this hill in the underground subway and laughing. I remember having fun. Then there was a beautiful, magnificent beach behind us and I felt this intense peace radiating toward us, coming from the beach. *Fun and peace with Z? Is this what the dream means, God? Tell me.*

∞

I was just on the phone with Z for two hours... I feel so at ease with him. He is safe and calming for me. His love for the Lord and for me is amazing. I pray God's will is done and into love we may fall...

∞

So, I'm being courted by Zander and it's like nothing I've ever experienced with a man before. His respect and love for me is so beautiful... so godly. On Friday he came up to see me dance hip-hop and the Brooklyn Tabernacle. Then we went to get something to eat... I was so exhausted but he is always so understanding of my tiredness from ministry. I feel bad when he comes up on a weekend when it's my trying-to-relax time and I'm always so out of it. But apparently we still make good conversation!

∞

I was just reading in Ephesians about a man and a wife becoming one flesh and the great mystery of that. I felt strongly the Lord assuring me that I am ready. I just kept hearing that; *"I am ready, I am ready."*

∞

God visited me last night. It was so sweet. He came and ministered to *me*. I stopped what I was doing (the dishes) and dropped to the floor. I begged Him not to go. I love Him so much. This was assurance to me that I am in His will. *I love You so much, Jesus.*

∞

Back to Africa

South Africa and Mozambique

I love sleeping in the South African stillness and beauty. Last night I dreamt about a girl who was screaming and slamming a door in my face. I shoved the door back open and began yelling and defending my cause. I can only come to the conclusion that she was an evil spirit warning me that we were not welcome.

Coming to Iris Harvest School of Missions was a dream I had over a year ago. An intern we had at Teen Challenge told me about it and said I should look into going since I am so crazy about Jesus. So I did. I saw the pictures of the orphans on their website and immediately yearned to be there.

I brought along Brandi on this trip. She is a T.C. graduate and I was honored to see her go through the whole program at Brooklyn and am so proud of her perseverance to chase after Jesus!

∞

I told a couple girls my testimony during rice and beans last night. They told me I was pure and innocent and that they would have never guessed my past. God is truly making me brand new. I am not who I used to be. Then we met with our small-groups and danced and played games! It was so fun to dance with the African people!

∞

Wow! Praise God! I was just at the Pemba beach here in Mozambique and got to share my story with some other missionaries who came from all over the world. Then God sent people to me. Jaquin was the first one- he is seventeen and turned away from the Muslim religion and gave his life to Jesus. God gave him the English language supernaturally awhile ago and that blew my mind! I saw Jesus in his eyes... he is beautiful.

Then four children came to me and I was already feeling the presence of God from speaking with Jaquin. So I asked the children if they knew Jesus, but they couldn't understand me because they spoke the Makua language. So I asked Jaquin to interpret. The children said they didn't know who Jesus was. So I grabbed my Bible and opened up to John, chapter three and read it to them. They listened intently. Then I explained who Jesus was and that He lives in my heart and loves me because I am His daughter. I asked them if they wanted Jesus to come into their heart and be their Father. They said an enthusiastic, "Yes." So I prayed for them all and touched their heads and hearts and blessed them in Jesus' name. They shouted, "Yay!"

I took a picture with them cuz they are so beautiful and I wanted to remember that moment forever.

∞

I was just at the beach, the Indian ocean, washing my hair and was about to leave to go back to the missionary base when a little girl ran up to hug me! She didn't talk at all and I tried to communicate in all three languages that are used around here; English, Portuguese and Makua. But she still didn't speak and she held on tightly to me and kept looking up at me with these sparkling, brown eyes. She was so sweet and I just kept embracing her.

When it was time to go she wouldn't let her eyes off me. Then she fell to the ground as the other missionary girls I was with kept telling me, "Come on, Mariah, we have to get back to the base."

But she just kept staring at me as she cuddled into the warm sand.

Ugh... my heart, my heart, my heart. My heart felt like it was being ripped apart.

I immediately thought of God- that must be how it feels for Him too. I just wanted to take her with me, go back and pick her up and tell her that I love her...

∞

At dinner tonight some girls were asking me about my life and Zander came up. Every time he comes up in conversation all the girls are always so excited and in shock of our story. The more I tell it, the more I believe that this relationship really is from God.

One of the girls said to me, "So is this time away from him a confirmation for you?"

I replied, "Yes it is, I suppose, because I actually miss him. It's not like we are growing apart... I feel we are growing together during this time."

∞

I just had the most amazing tome worshipping God through dance with three other Jesus-lovers! We had a creative arts meeting and I was talking with the dancers and felt we should pray together. So we did and then we went to the hut where we have school and we praised God through dance for like an hour.

At the following creative arts meeting I was spontaneously elected to be the dance leader of the school. Me? Okay! I am excited to see how God wants to express Himself through our movement... *give me wisdom and creativity, Lord!*

∞

I can't even describe today. The heart of God and the mind of Christ were both planted in me and I wept, I wept, I wept. I wept so much that snot was coming out of my nose and my ribs were shaking uncontrollably. God gave me the gift of being able to feel *His* compassion for the lost and orphaned children.

Heidi Baker (the Iris Harvest School of Missions founder) was ministering in class today and she was going to talk about something in the book of Philippians, but then felt the Holy Spirit wanted to minister to us. She led us in a time of deep prayer and focus on Jesus.

I was determined to touch the hem of Jesus' garment today. But I got so much more than personal healing. I experienced the heart of God- how He hurts for the orphans, the lost and the sick- there are no words to describe it.

God gave me a vision of the children all over the world who are hungry, being raped, being sold... oh my heart.

My heart is broke for God.

∞

I am getting so homesick! This life here is beautiful, breathtaking, slow and fulfilling- but I miss my Teen Challenge family. I miss my mom, dad and siblings. And I miss Zander. I want to fully absorb this experience so I'm trusting God that He has my life figured out and I can just rest.

Everyday my revelations of God's fatherly heart are growing deeper and deeper.

Yesterday, I was telling Lauren, my housemate, about what God has audibly spoken to me a few years ago and I got encouraged again as I told her what He said, *"You were what you were- but you are who you are through Me."*

AMEN! And that's who I am! No more striving, no more human effort or being anything other than Jesus' daughter. He doesn't ask for much from us... so why do we make it so complicated sometimes?

∞

Only a few weeks left of this amazing time in my favorite place- *Africa*.

God keeps speaking to me three things that I need to take with me for the rest of my life: He wants me to live an abundant life, a full life. Secondly, He wants me to live a life of joy, to be joyful in all situations. And finally, He wants me to abide in Him and He will remain in me. That is what He's saying He wants from me... to live a joyful and abundant life abiding in Him.

∞

Today we had a foot washing ceremony. I was washing a Mozambican pastor's feet and began crying as I prayed for him. I cleaned and dried his feet carefully. Then he began to wash my feet and pray for me.

I just sobbed... the tears kept coming. I was so humbled to receive a foot washing from him. After we were done all I could do was sit there and weep and rest in the arms of my Father.

∞

This weekend I spent the night in a village hut in the depths of poverty and dirt. It was so fun! We stayed with a Mozambican momma who had four grandchildren living with her. I got to carry the youngest, who is two years old, around on my back with a capulana (African skirt that doubles as a baby-carrier). I also got to rock him to sleep and put him on his cot. The village kids walked us home the following afternoon and the youngest boy started crying when we separated. Oh, my heart... I love these children. Someday, I want to take in orphans.

∞

Last night we were watching Nefarious on a drop-cloth underneath the stars. Afterward I just laid there asking God what I could do for Him. He told me I was asking that question like I was still a prostitute. That I was treating Him like someone who just wanted something from me. Whoa. He proceeded to ask me what it was the He could do for me. And I, taken aback by that question, hesitatingly, but curiously, asked Him for a shooting star. A few seconds went by and then there it went! A beautiful shooting star, just for me. *I love You, Jesus. Thank You for the shooting star and that I don't need to sell myself to You.*

∞

I was just asked to create a graduation dance- I am up for the task! Today's dance practice was so exhilarating and encouraging! I love to do this! We are almost done with the dance and it is going to be awesome. *Thank You Jesus, we dance for You!*

∞

Dance practice today was so fun! There are fourteen of us now and I am absolutely drowning in joy as I lead them. I always start the practice with an exhortation and explain the power of dance... that it is not about technique or performance- but that it's about our heart and passion for worshipping God.

One of the dancers asked me after practice about my life. She said she sensed I was very full and that I must've lived a crazy life. She said I was a treasure and then prayed for me. *God, I pray that You will send the dancers! I want, crave and desire to create this dance for You glory. I am passionate about this. Your will be done as it is in heaven. I love You forever.*

∞

Leaving this land in a few days... I am so excited for Brooklyn pizza! I am full of sorrow to leave this place but also happy to go home to Teen Challenge. I don't know if God will have me there forever, but I fully trust Him when He is ready to release me. I also trust God if I marry Zander... I trust Him completely that He will take care of me. *I thank You a million times for giving me this gift of being with You so intimately. I love You so much and can't wait to spend the rest of my life and all eternity with You, God.*

∞

Back Home… and Engaged!

I returned home to Brooklyn only to leave again to Rochester, NY to visit my family. It was so nice seeing everyone. They all asked me a bunch of questions about

Africa. Oh yea, and I brought along Zander too! My family loved him. I couldn't wait to see him and give him a hug.

The other night Zander and I left my grandma's house and went to the town of Hamlin. I wanted to show him where I grew up. I took him to Hamlin Beach also and it was perfect timing because the sun was just setting. While we were at the beach he proposed!! It was so beautifully awkward- just like Zander. The sunset sky and the water waving in the ocean brought with it a heavy sense of peace in our midst. I love how God drew the clouds and painted the sea.

After a choppy conversation and some mumbling from Zander, he finally spit out the question he was trying to ask and I replied with, *"Are you sure?!"* It was the obvious question to ask someone who just proposed, right?

And he said, *"Yes. I want to marry you and spend forever loving you."*

So I hugged him tightly and said, *"Yes, Zander."*

∞

Africa Calling... Jos, Nigeria

Was back in Brooklyn for a few weeks, only to leave again to lead a mission's trip to Nigeria! Yes!

Zander went to work back down in Virginia after our trip to Rochester, but then came back up to Brooklyn to lead a team to

Jamaica Teen Challenge! We were both leading teams from Brooklyn Teen Challenge at the same time in different countries.

So I am here in Jos, Nigeria. God is preparing the way for us every step we take. We had a visa issue, a plane issue and a physical pain issue amongst the teammates- but God keeps making the impossible possible! Nigeria is very different than Swaziland and Mozambique. This country is more like South Africa because it is very well-to-do. Hopefully we can get out into the slums and the bush! God has been giving me the blessing of watching my team members experience this for the first time...

I love it. I am so at peace. But I miss Zander terribly.

∞

Today I have such a migraine, but I'm pressing through. Yesterday I got to go into a dark brothel. I was in tears before I spoke to those girls just thinking of how blessed I am to be freed from prostitution. God is so good. I love being the light in a dark place. I'll never forget that experience. I'm grateful to have brought Krystel with me. Krystel is our women's home leader at Teen Challenge. Her heart is so pure and she's never seen anything like that in her life. I love seeing people grow in Christ as they branch out of their comfort zone and leap out on faith. What a joyful day!

We head back to Brooklyn in a few days... sad to leave Africa but excited to see family and Zander.

∞

I can hardly believe it... Ashley, the dance leader at the Brooklyn Tabernacle just asked if I would be willing to share my testimony and dance during their first ever dance ministry production! Me?! What a blessing and an honor to share my story yet again, but this time, in front of thousands of people. I am so grateful...

∞

end of entries

*Now this is not the end. It is not even the beginning of the end.
But it is, perhaps, the end of the beginning.*

∞Winston Churchill∞

The writer's block happened as a whirlwind of events took place in my life- hence the end of journal entries.

The whirlwind of events twirled around to create; a happy childhood, mental illness, suicide attempts, drug addiction and everything imaginable that goes with that; to life in rehabs and institutions. Then the whirlwind of new life, restoration and freedom at the Walter Hoving Home, then Brooklyn Teen Challenge and then the Teen Challenges in Africa! Among which I danced all along the way... even to the stage of the Brooklyn Tabernacle.

There were the whirlwinds of falling in love! Speaking of which, Zander and I are now married. I'm going to risk sounding cliché and just say it- we are *happily* married.

I left Brooklyn, Teen Challenge and everything I've ever known to be married to Zander and move to Southern Virginia.

... a whirlwind of change, indeed.

Our wedding was simple, beautiful and meaningful. I wore a long-sleeved hippie inspired dress. And I dressed Zander up in a white bowtie with matching suspenders.

My boss, Don Wilkerson, married us and all of our close friends and relatives were there to witness our vow to one another.

Jesus was the guest of honor at our wedding and He continues to be the center of our marriage. That is why I can say to you; we are *happily* married. Not because our circumstances are perfect. And we have gotten into some struggles, trust me! But it is because we continue to daily seek God and pray for each other and *choose* to love the other person.

Two weeks after our wedding we got the privilege to lead a team from Brooklyn Teen Challenge to Germany! We went to help construct the Germany Teen Challenge Women's home! This was our honeymoon and we couldn't have asked for a better one. God supplied all of our needs and we even got to do a little sightseeing. It was a joy to serve and to see what God is doing throughout the world.

Zander got to take some of our honeymoon home with him, as he tripped and fell on a rock while he was hard at work and gashed his shin open. He had to get stitches, which he did not want to do, and he even wanted to keep working through his injury! I had to pull him away from working and convince him to go get it stitched up. Thankfully, he healed up nicely and now has a reminder of sentimental value- my warrior for God's Kingdom!

∞

As I sit here typing and munching on animal crackers, I am listening to my six month old steadily breathe through the baby monitor. I have a six month old! Me?! God has given me another chance at being a mother…

I don't deserve it.

That's the thing about God. He *is* love. He is graceful. He is forgiving. He is our Father... our Poppa. He's our Dad.

None of us deserve Him. And we cannot do anything to earn Him. That's grace.

We must only believe that He is... then we must *allow* Him to take care of the rest. And He will- in ways we simply cannot imagine.

∞

angels

Are not all ministering spirits sent to serve those who will inherit salvation?

∞Hebrews 1:14∞

I end my book with this chapter; in honor of those on earth who help others. And those who listen to the Holy Spirit by praying for someone or giving someone a nonjudgmental hug that may have had a treacherously long and lonely journey. To all of you who have picked me up and dusted me off-
Thank You.

When I was in Africa a missionary friend told me she saw two huge protector angels behind me. I had known and sensed these angels before, especially when I would come close to dying several times due to overdosing or the dangerous situations I put myself in.

I am so thankful for the way God has protected me throughout the years of risky behavior, suicide attempts and drug use. Did you know that God is concerned and protective of us?

Whether we choose to believe it or not; angels, demons and the spiritual realm are very real. Psalms 91:11 says, *"For he will command his angels concerning you to guard you in all your ways."*

There are other types of angels; the ones who are visible and have always been close to our hearts. I believe we as people can act as God's agents- protecting others and coming to help them by responding to a command from our Father.

There are a few different people in my life that I must give credit to for why I am still alive:

First, there is my mom and dad. They have spent endless sleepless nights worrying about where I was, tending to me and cleaning up my vomit. They have spent thousands of dollars for therapy treatments, hospital stays, medications, lawyers, car-crash expenses and much more. There were countless times they have been the victims of my crimes against them (stealing, lying, verbally abusing, etc.). Their selfless acts of love have shown me what being a parent is all about. I know I was not a good daughter... I know I was weak, sick and helplessly addicted. They had to witness the pain of slowly killing myself- but they never stopped fighting for me. I know I can never repay them for all they've done for me. But maybe I can- by living a healthy, joyful life... the life they always fought so hard for me to have.

Secondly, there is Katie Strizak. She has been my best friend since we were basically in diapers. Katie has never stopped speaking the truth of God's love into my life. She has also witnessed me almost kill myself many times but has remained the solid rock of a praying friend that I so desperately needed. She and her sister, Sarah, were the ones who gave me the information about the Walter Hoving Home. And for this I am forever grateful. I count their angel-like friendship and as a gift from God.

Thirdly, there are the nameless and faceless people in the medical profession. Although they may not be Christian- they all have the desire to help others. God uses people of all kinds to execute His will on earth. I cannot count the amount of times my life was saved due to these precious people... and in my eyes, angels.

Finally, there is my sweet husband. He has always treated me like nothing less than a princess. He continues to save my tainted view on men as he leads me into the arms of Jesus all the time. I still struggle with things from my past, especially sexual trauma, but he remains my praying and loving partner through it all. For this, I thank God that He has sent me one of His angels to live with for the rest of my earthly life.

∞

About the Author

Mariah Noelle Freeman was born and raised in Rochester, NY. She was a lively, curious child who immersed herself in many outlets such as dance, music, writing, theatre, sports and with having a lot of friends. She was raised in the church setting but never fully grasped how much God loved her. Mariah walked away from God in her early teens and embraced a life of rebellion, sin and ultimately was thrown into the slimy hands of addiction and mental illness. Her addiction and illness were so severe that it landed her in many hospitals with mental hygiene arrests and drug overdoses. She was at the mercy of medications, doctors, drugs and her worst enemy- her very self.

She finally gave up control when she was turned down during a prostitution job due to her ragged, heroin-induced appearance and her dirty living environment in a garage. It was then that she pulled out the information on the Walter Hoving Home that she hid away for years, and began the process of admittance into their one year program.

She has let God take all of her sicknesses and received His love in place of the void she once had. She has been dramatically and deliberately set free through the power of Jesus Christ.

Mariah now volunteers at a crisis pregnancy center, counseling women who are faced with an unplanned pregnancy. She also continues to assist the president of Brooklyn Teen Challenge as well as help out the staff when needed. Additionally, Mariah enjoys leading a women's Bible study in her home.

She lives in Southern Virginia with her husband Zander and daughter, Nova Grace.

∞

Swaziland, Africa

Mozambique, Africa

Nigeria, Africa

Wedding Day!

Germany Missions Trip/ Honeymoon

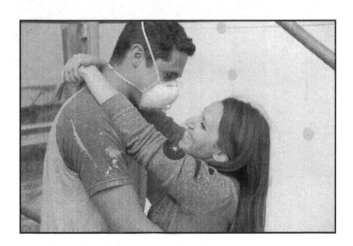

Brooklyn Teen Challenge team at Germany
Teen Challenge

from heroin to heaven

Mariah would love to hear from you:

sinnersaved@live.com

Or write her at:

340 Halifax Street

Danville, VA 24540

Please don't wait another day. Call if you need help:

The Walter Hoving Home

(Christian rehabilitation program for women)

40 Walter Hoving Road

Garrison, NY 10524

845.424.3693

Brooklyn Teen Challenge

(Christian rehabilitation program for men and women)

444 Clinton Avenue

Brooklyn, NY 11238

718.789.1414

Made in the USA
Lexington, KY
22 November 2015